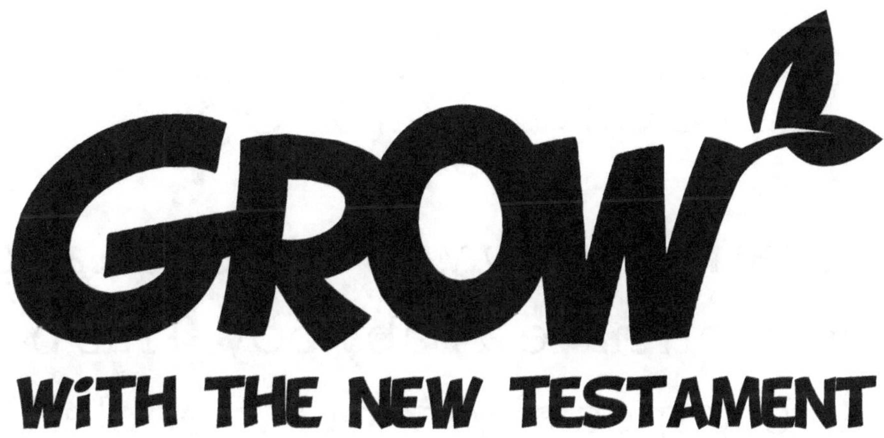


# GROW
## WITH THE NEW TESTAMENT

**STORIES BY ASHLEY HUDSON**
**ILLUSTRATIONS BY JASON HUTTON**
**EDITED BY MICHAEL WHITWORTH**



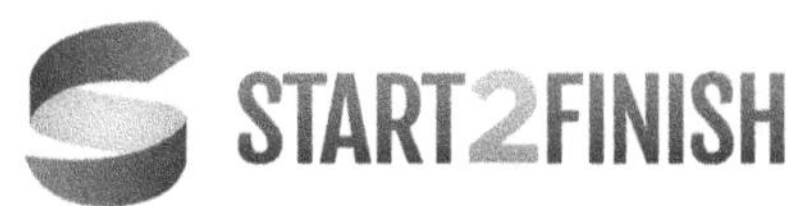

# AN ANGEL VISITS MARY

## LUKE 1:26-38

A woman named Mary was told by an angel that she would soon have a baby boy. This baby boy would be very special to a lot of people. She was to name the baby "Jesus." Jesus was God's Son, our Savior. She told her soon-to-be-husband, Joseph, about the special baby, and they were both happy and thankful that God chose them to take care of baby Jesus.

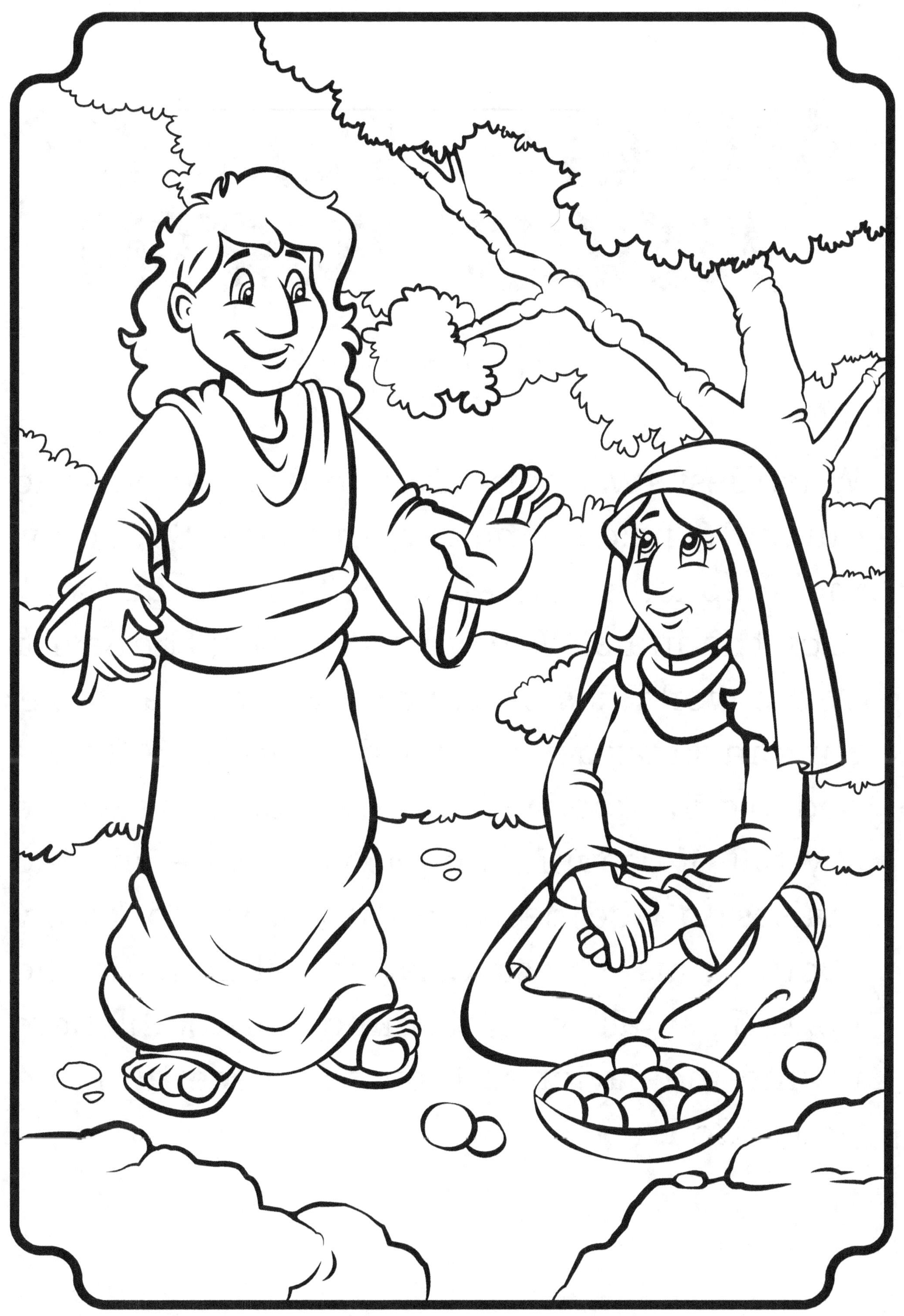

# ANGELS TELL OF JESUS' BIRTH

## LUKE 2:8-20

When Jesus was born, shepherds were working out in the field taking care of sheep. Suddenly, the shepherds saw an angel! The angel said, "Don't be afraid! We have good news! The Savior of the world has been born! He is in a stable, lying in a manger, wrapped in cloths." After he had told the good news, the shepherds saw the sky full of beautiful angels who were singing praises to God because they were so happy about Jesus. Guess what the shepherds did next? They all went running into Bethlehem to find the Savior so they could see him and praise God.

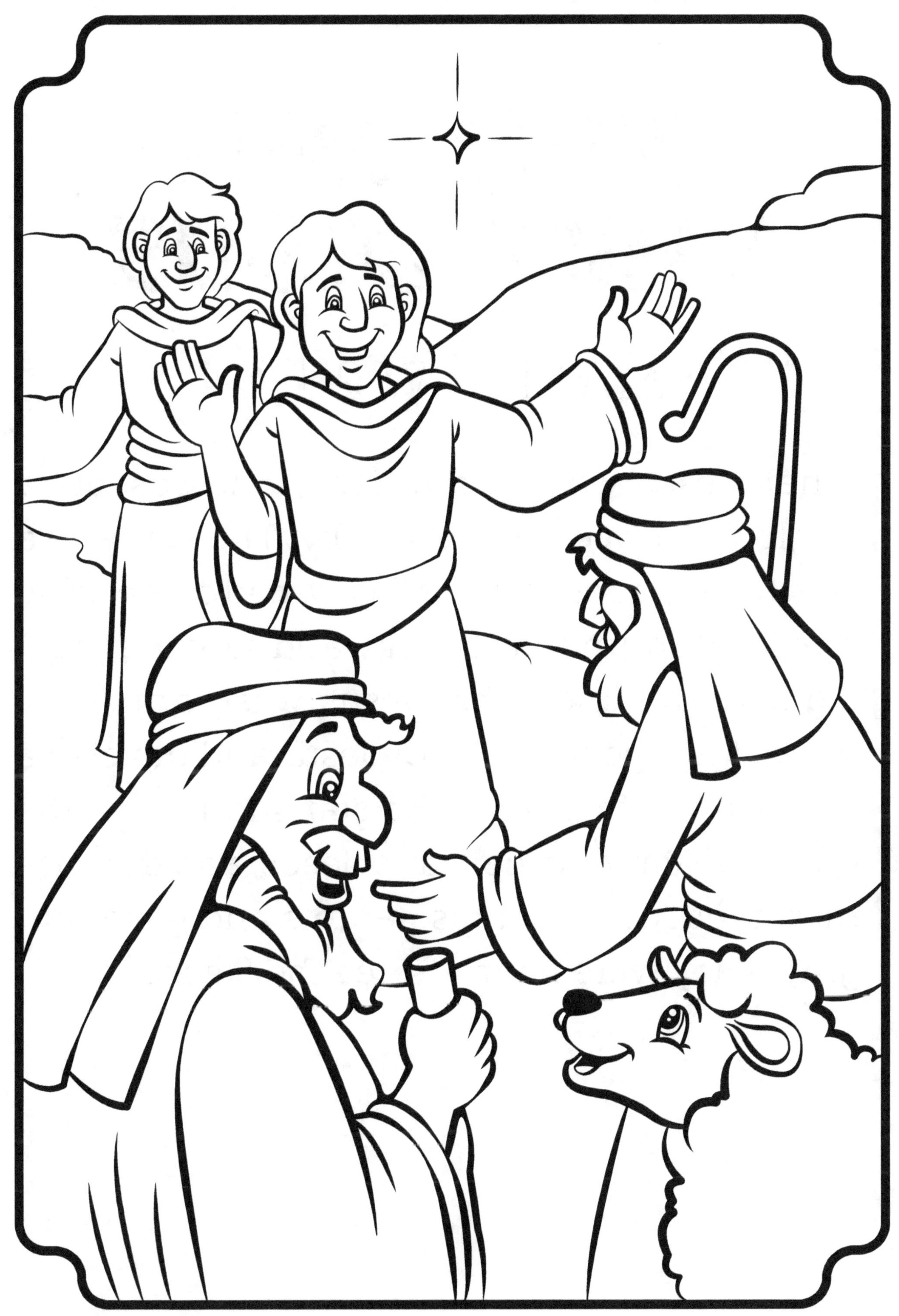

# WISE MEN VISIT JESUS

## MATTHEW 2:1-12

When Jesus was born to Mary and Joseph, a bright star appeared in the sky. The star was a sign to the people that the Savior had come! Wise men looked up into the sky and saw the great big star and knew that Jesus was born. They packed up special gifts for Jesus and traveled a long way to find him. The star shone over the house of Mary, Joseph, and Jesus, and the wise men met Jesus and his parents and gave him gifts. They were happy to see the Savior.

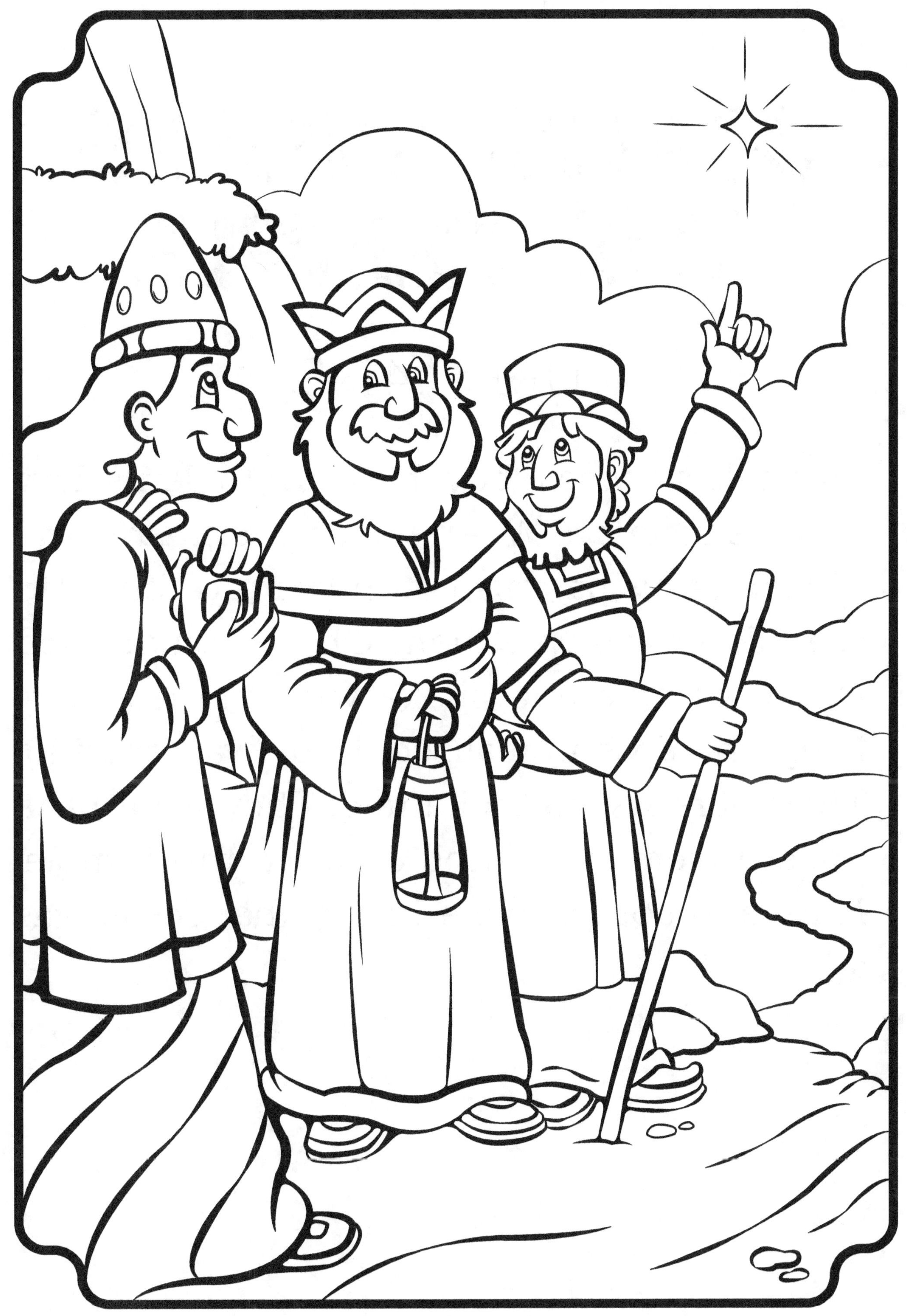

# JESUS VISITS THE TEMPLE

## LUKE 2:41-53

When Jesus was a boy, he went to Jerusalem for a celebration. When it was over, Mary and Joseph, Jesus' parents, left and forgot to check to see if Jesus was with them. Oh no! Jesus stayed in the Temple and spoke with the teachers. Mary and Joseph realized Jesus was missing! They were so sad and afraid! They went back to Jerusalem and found Jesus in the Temple. Mary and Joseph were happy that Jesus was safe.

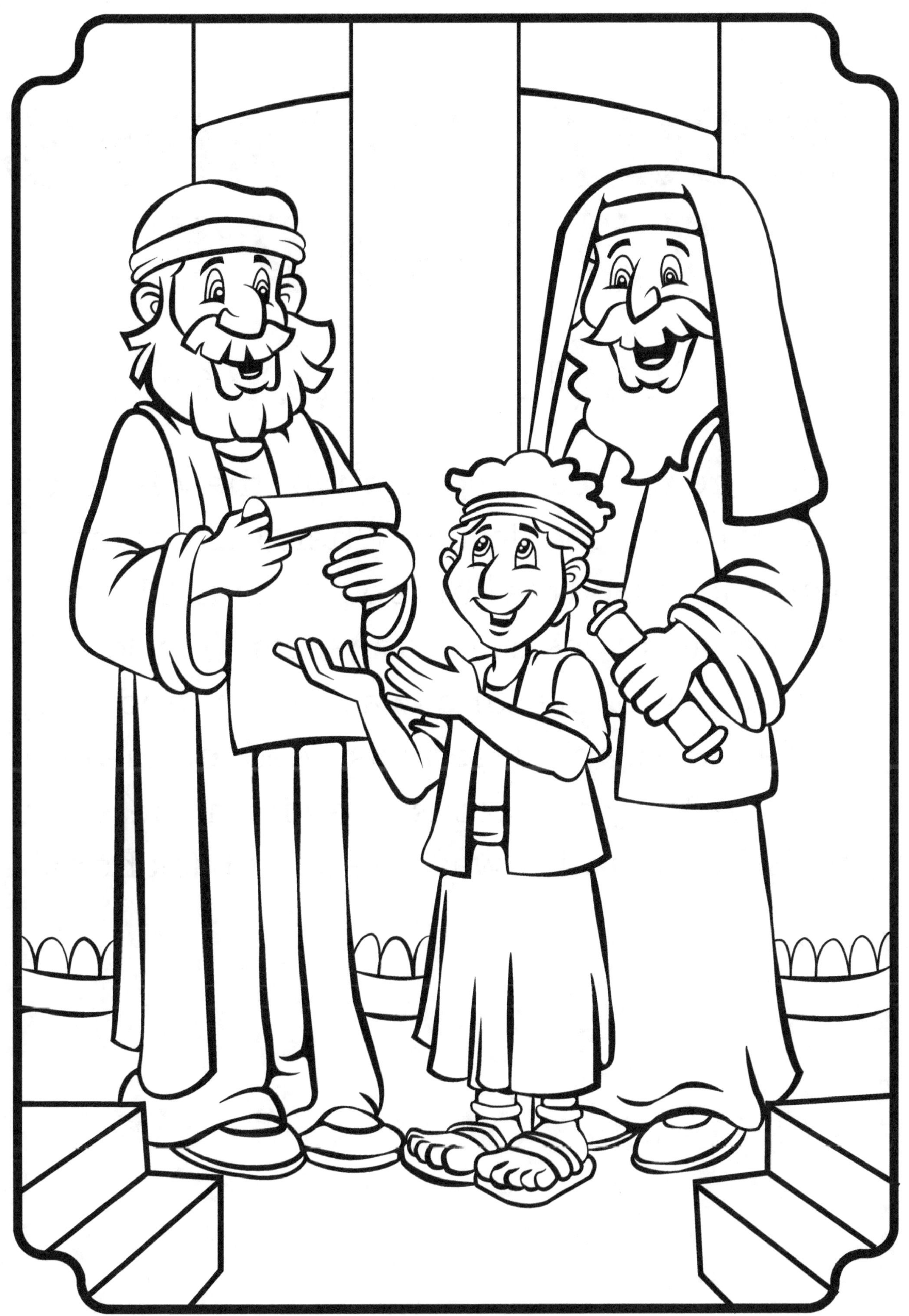

# JESUS ESCAPES TO EGYPT

## MATTHEW 2:13-23

Do you remember talking about the wise men who came to see Jesus? When they came to town, they asked the king about Jesus. The king was jealous of Jesus. An angel came to Joseph and told him the king was angry, and they needed to escape. Joseph listened to the angel and took Mary and Jesus away in the desert to live in Egypt until it was safe to go back home.

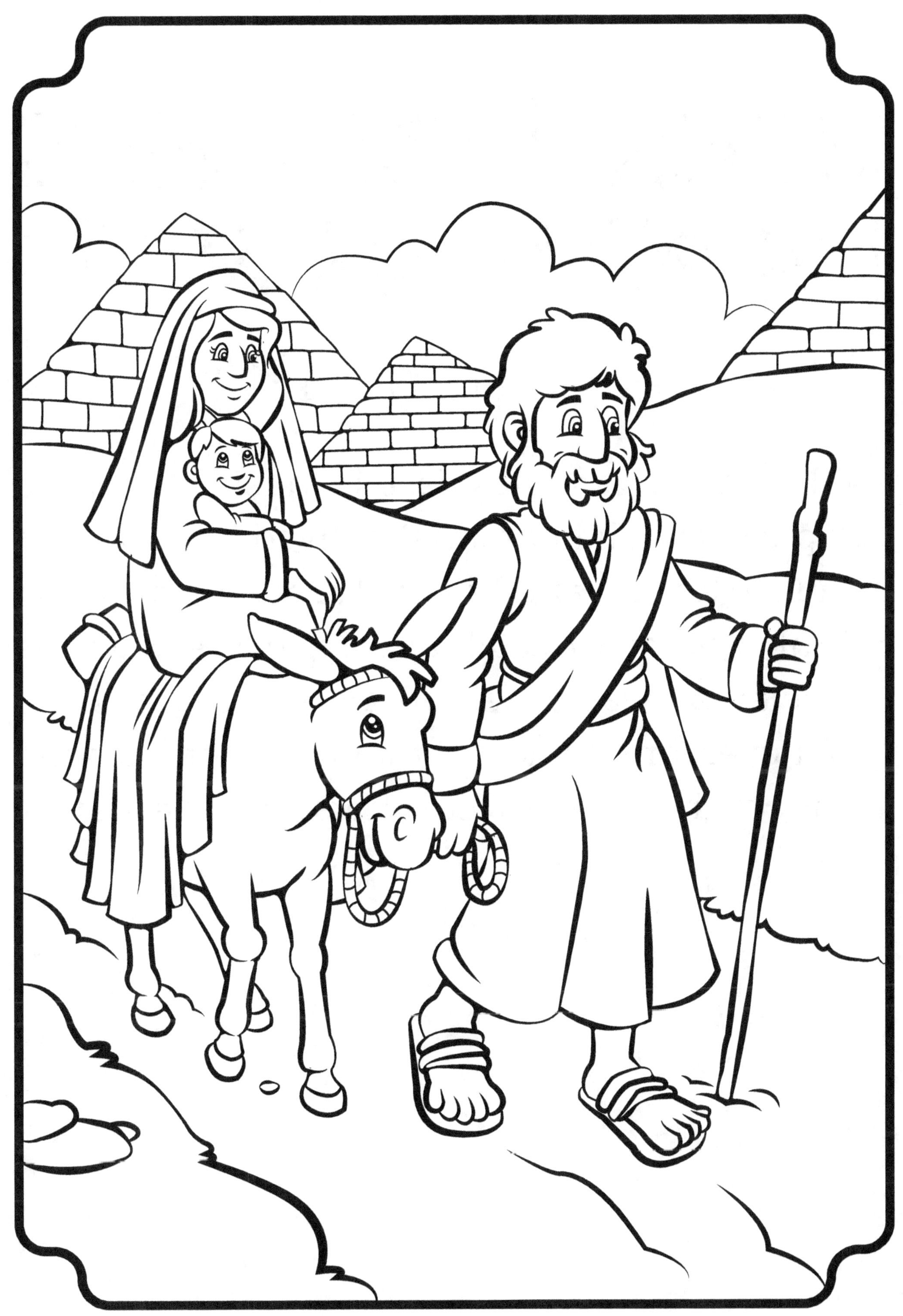

# JOHN PREACHES ABOUT JESUS

## MATTHEW 3:1-12

John the Baptist was Jesus' cousin. John the Baptist was a hairy man that lived in the desert and ate locusts and honey. He ate bugs! I don't think I want to eat bugs. John the Baptist's special job was to tell others about Jesus. He told everyone he knew that Jesus, the Savior, was coming! We can tell others about Jesus too!

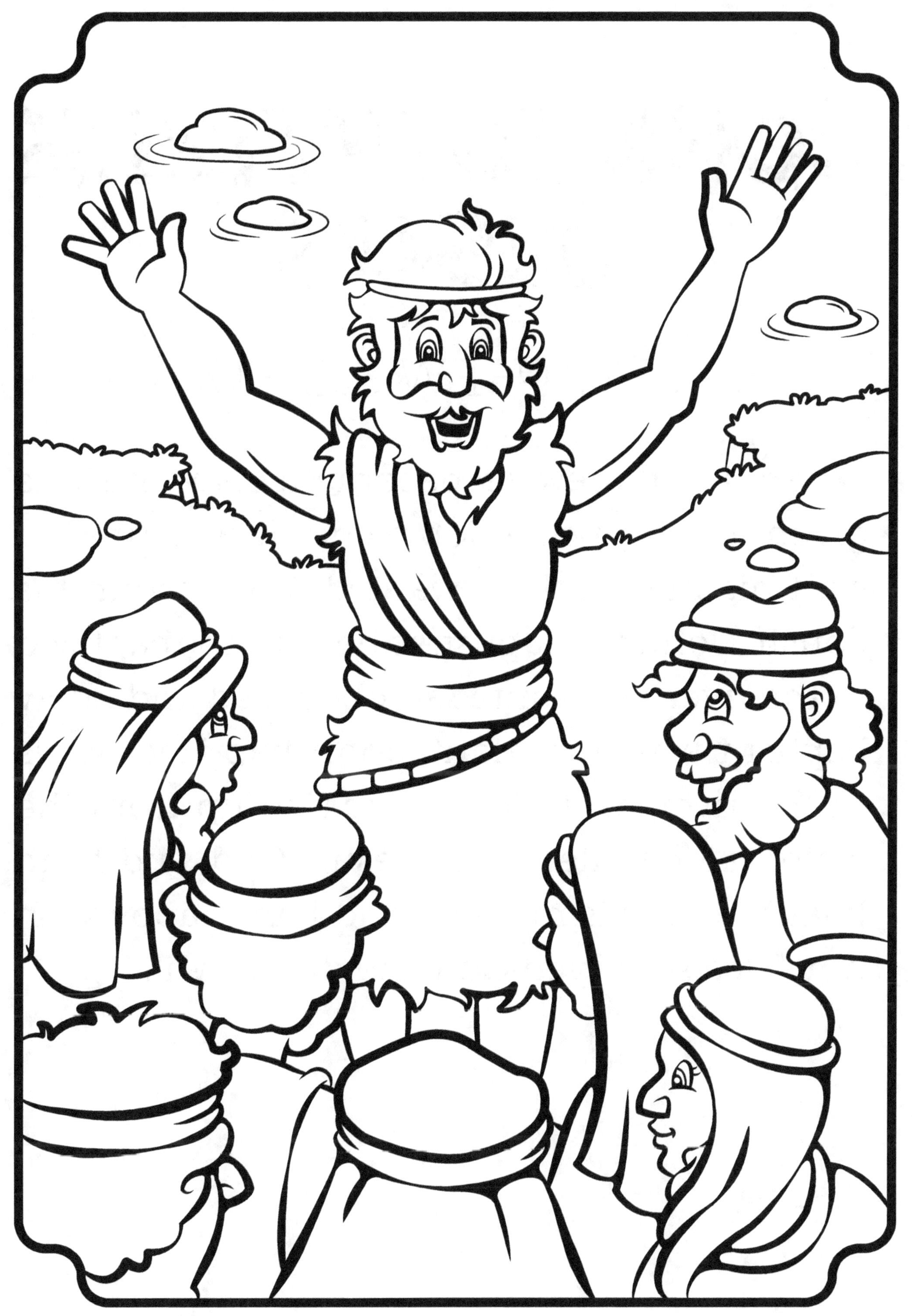

# JOHN BAPTIZES JESUS

## MATTHEW 3:13-17

When Jesus grew to become a man, he was given a very special job to do. It was time to start his ministry! He wanted to visit with his cousin, John the Baptist, so he could be baptized in the river. He wanted to obey God and knew baptism was important. John baptized Jesus in the river, and when he came up from the water, a dove flew over Jesus. God said from heaven, "This is my Son, and I am happy with him." Jesus obeyed God and did his will.

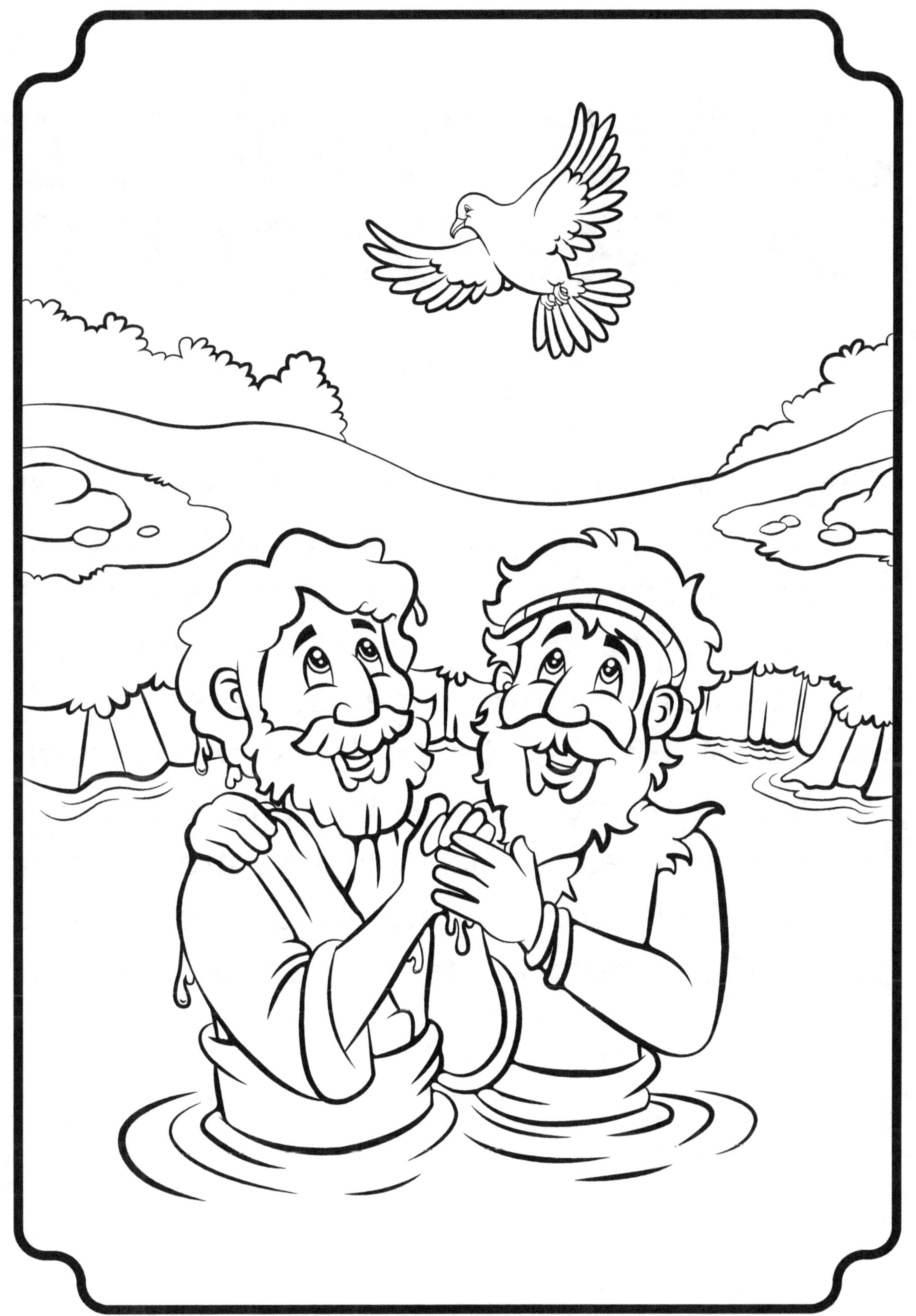

# JESUS TEMPTED IN THE DESERT

## MATTHEW 4:1-11

Jesus was in the desert to fast and pray. To fast means that you do not eat anything, even if you're hungry! The devil came to Jesus while in the desert and tried to make him eat food. He told Jesus to turn stones into bread. Jesus said, "No!" He knew the devil was trying to trick him to do wrong. The devil tried to trick Jesus two more times, but Jesus stayed strong. After the devil left, God sent angels to Jesus to take care of him. Jesus resisted the devil and obeyed God.

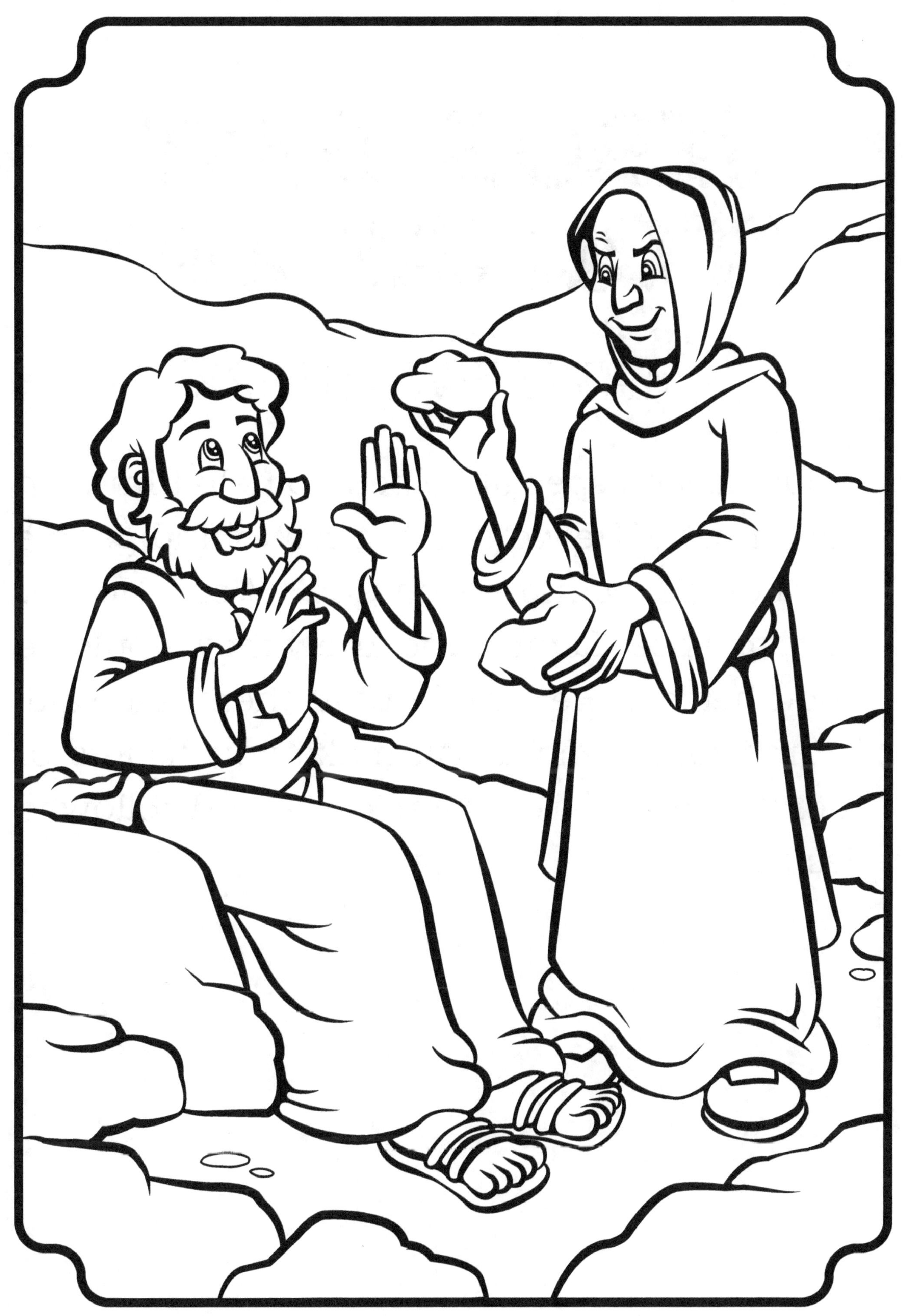

# JESUS SAYS "FOLLOW ME"

## MATTHEW 4:18-22

Jesus needed special helpers to help him with his ministry. He went to the sea to find people that could help him teach God's Word. He saw men in a boat fishing and knew they would be good helpers. He called out to them and said, "Come follow me! I will make you fishers of men!" The men left their boats and followed Jesus.

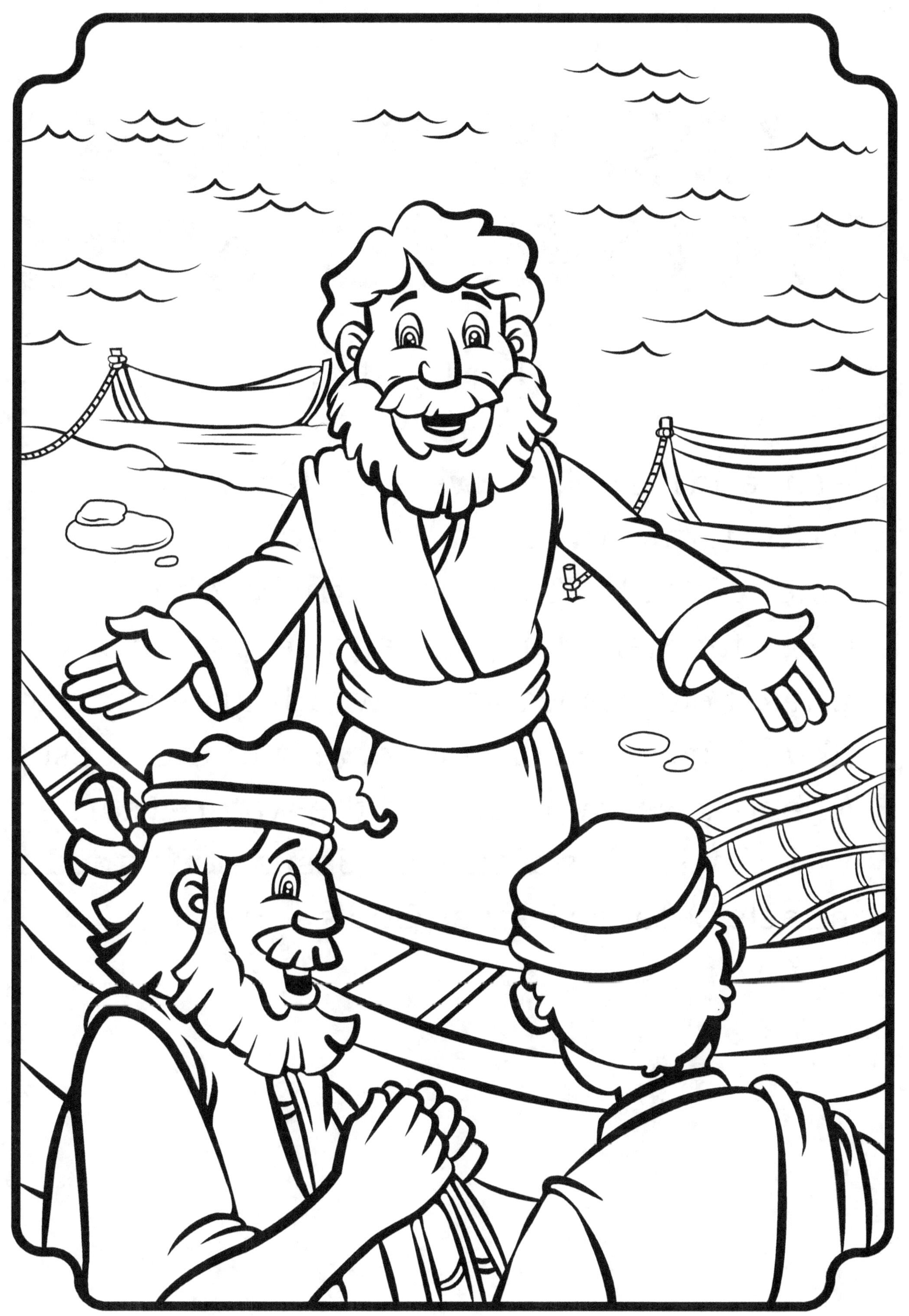

# JESUS TURNS WATER TO WINE

## JOHN 2:1-11

Jesus and his helpers were invited to a wedding feast. During the feast, the people ran out of wine to drink. They didn't know what to do! Jesus' mother, Mary, came to Jesus and asked him to help. Jesus told the wedding servants to fill up jugs of water and serve it to the guests. When the servants poured the water, it turned into wine! It was a miracle! Jesus performed a miracle because he was God's son.

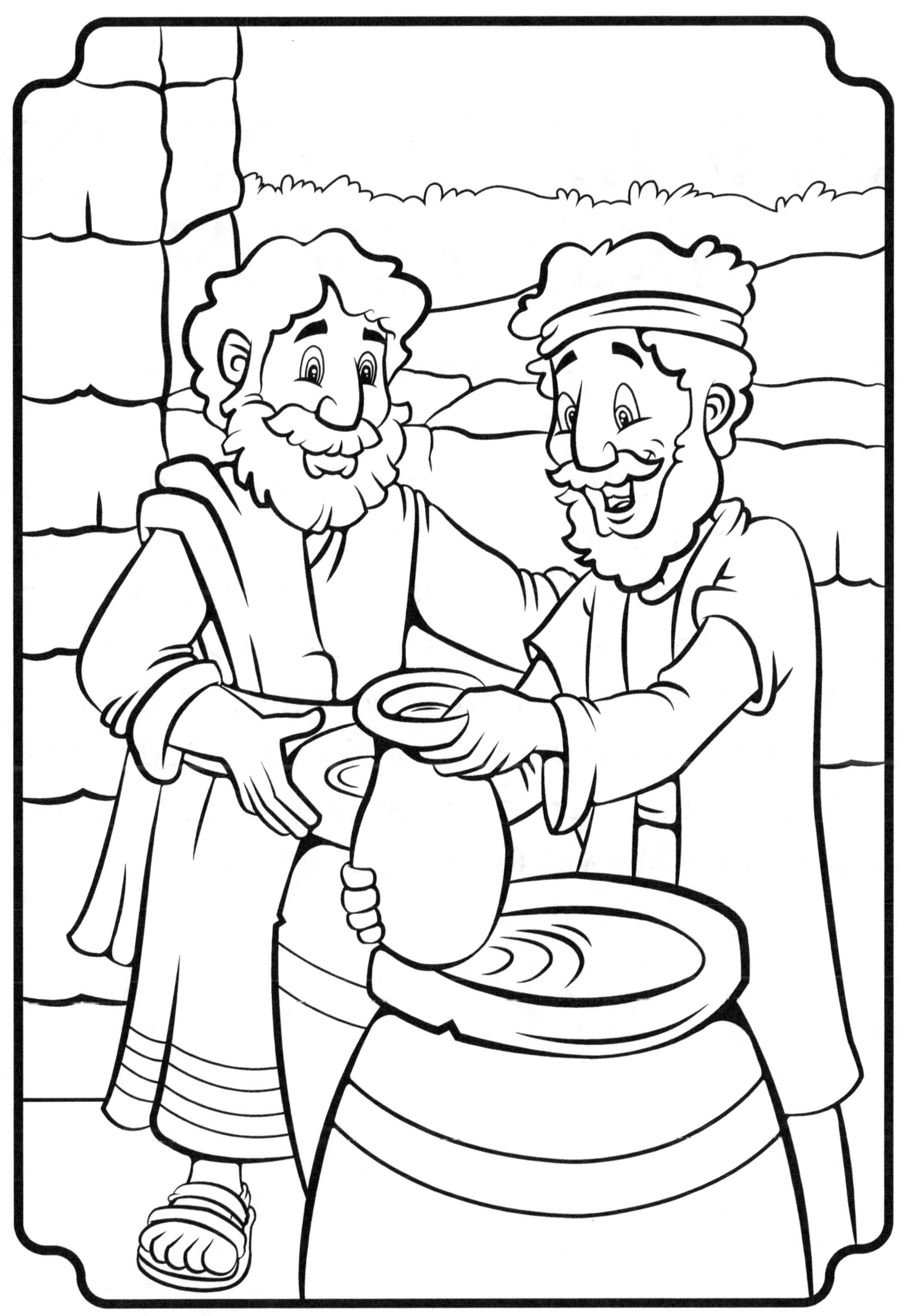

# JESUS TALKS TO NICODEMUS

## JOHN 3:1-21

While preaching to others about God, Jesus met a man named Nicodemus. Can you say, Nicodemus? Nicodemus was a teacher who wanted to hear more about God's Word. He met with Jesus when it was night-time and Jesus and Nicodemus talked about God's love. Nicodemus listened to Jesus and asked good questions. He was learning from Jesus!

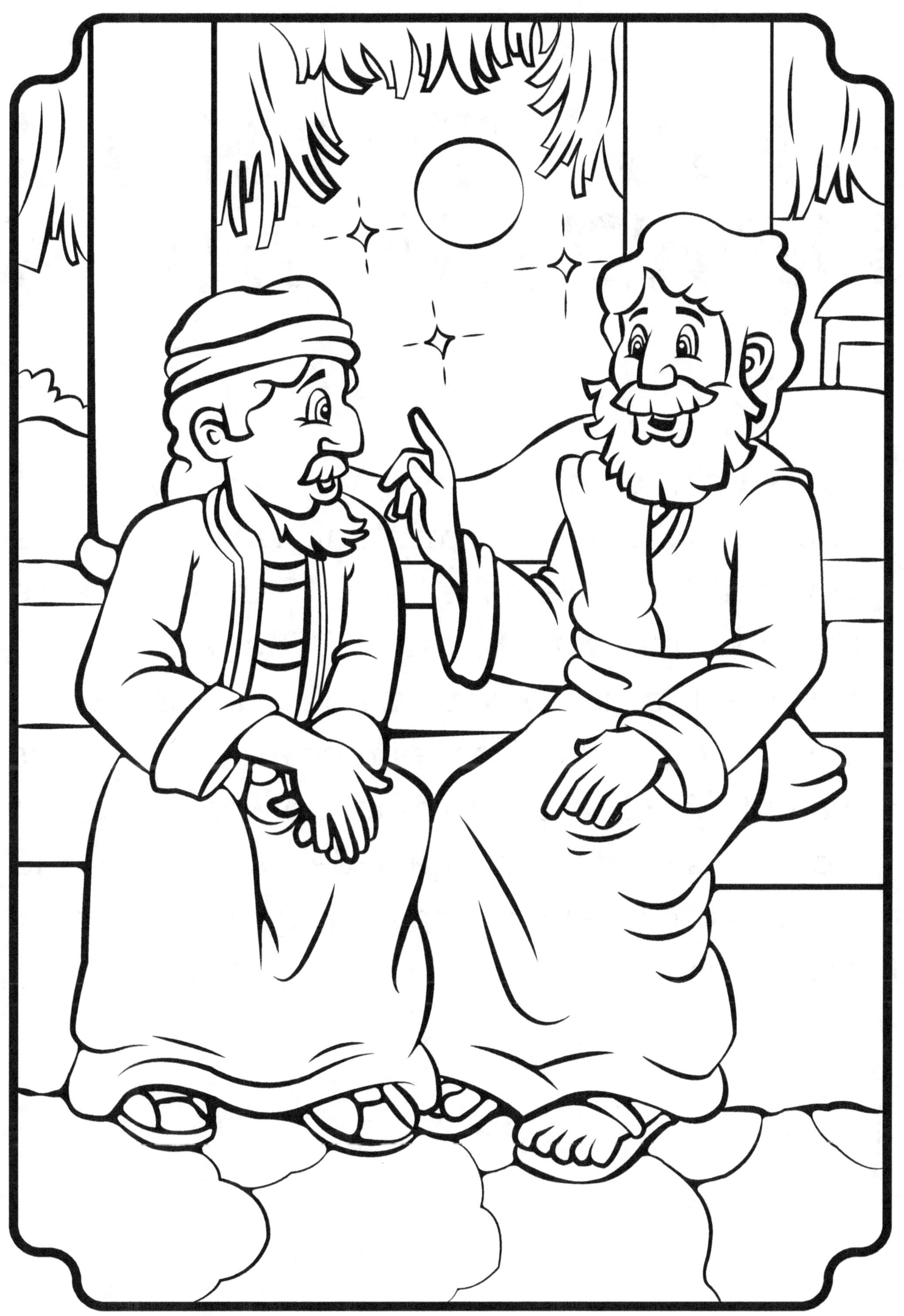

# JESUS TALKS TO SAMARITAN WOMAN

## JOHN 4:1-42

Jesus went on a very long walk and was tired and thirsty. He saw a drinking well and met a woman there. He asked her, "Can you please get me some water to drink?" The woman was surprised Jesus talked to her because she didn't have any friends. She was nice and gave Jesus water to drink. Jesus told her he was the son of God. This made her happy. Jesus was a friend to the woman, and she told everyone she knew about Jesus.

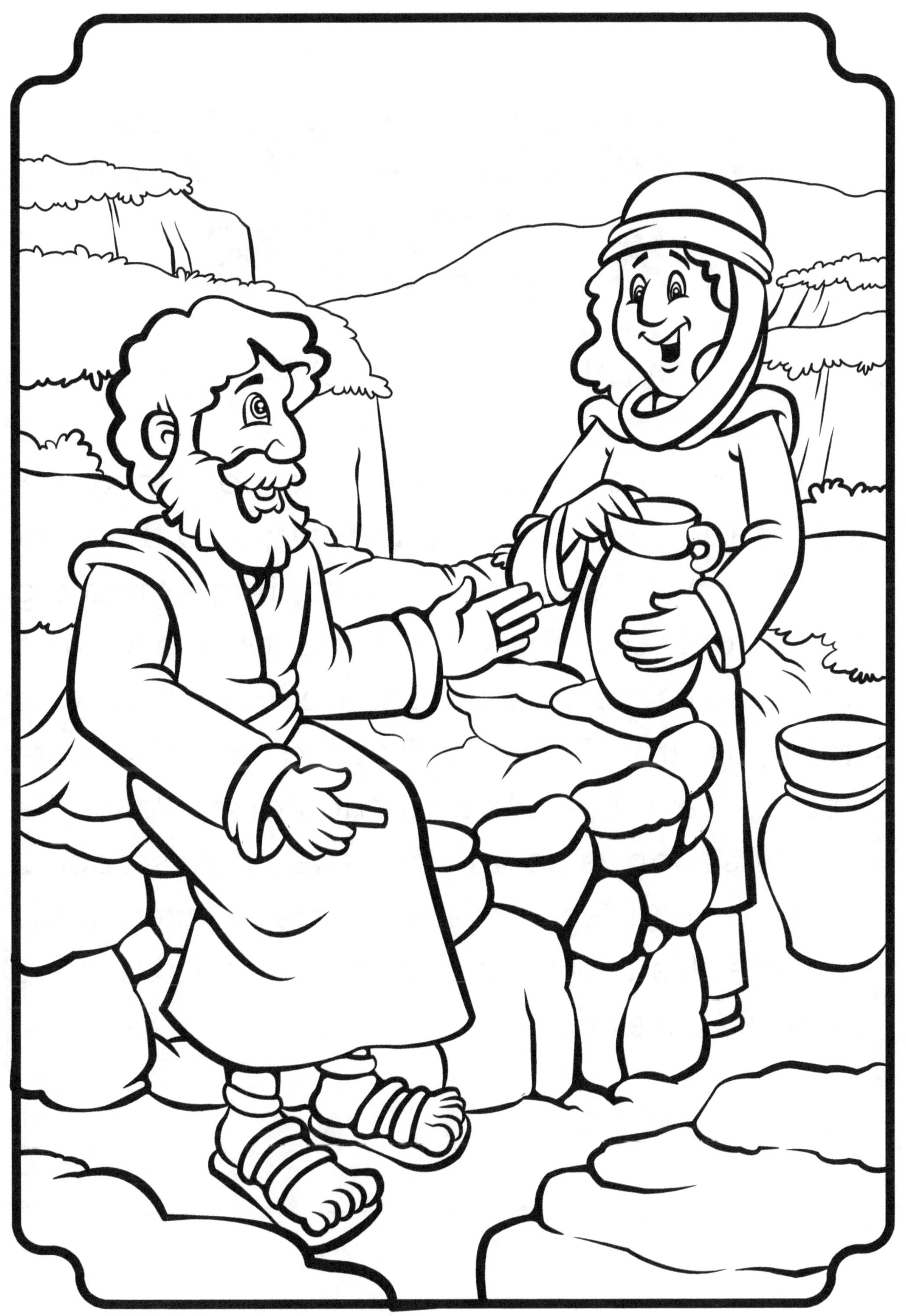

# JESUS CALMS A STORM

## MATTHEW 8:23-27

Jesus and his friends got on a boat to travel across the sea. Jesus went down into the boat to take a nap. While he was sleeping, a great big storm rocked the boat back and forth, back and forth. Jesus' friends were scared! The boat was going to sink! They cried out to Jesus to wake up! Jesus awoke and said to the storm, "Peace, be still. " As soon as he said this, the storm stopped! Just like that! Jesus' friends were amazed at his miracle. Jesus was able to do miracles because he was God's Son.

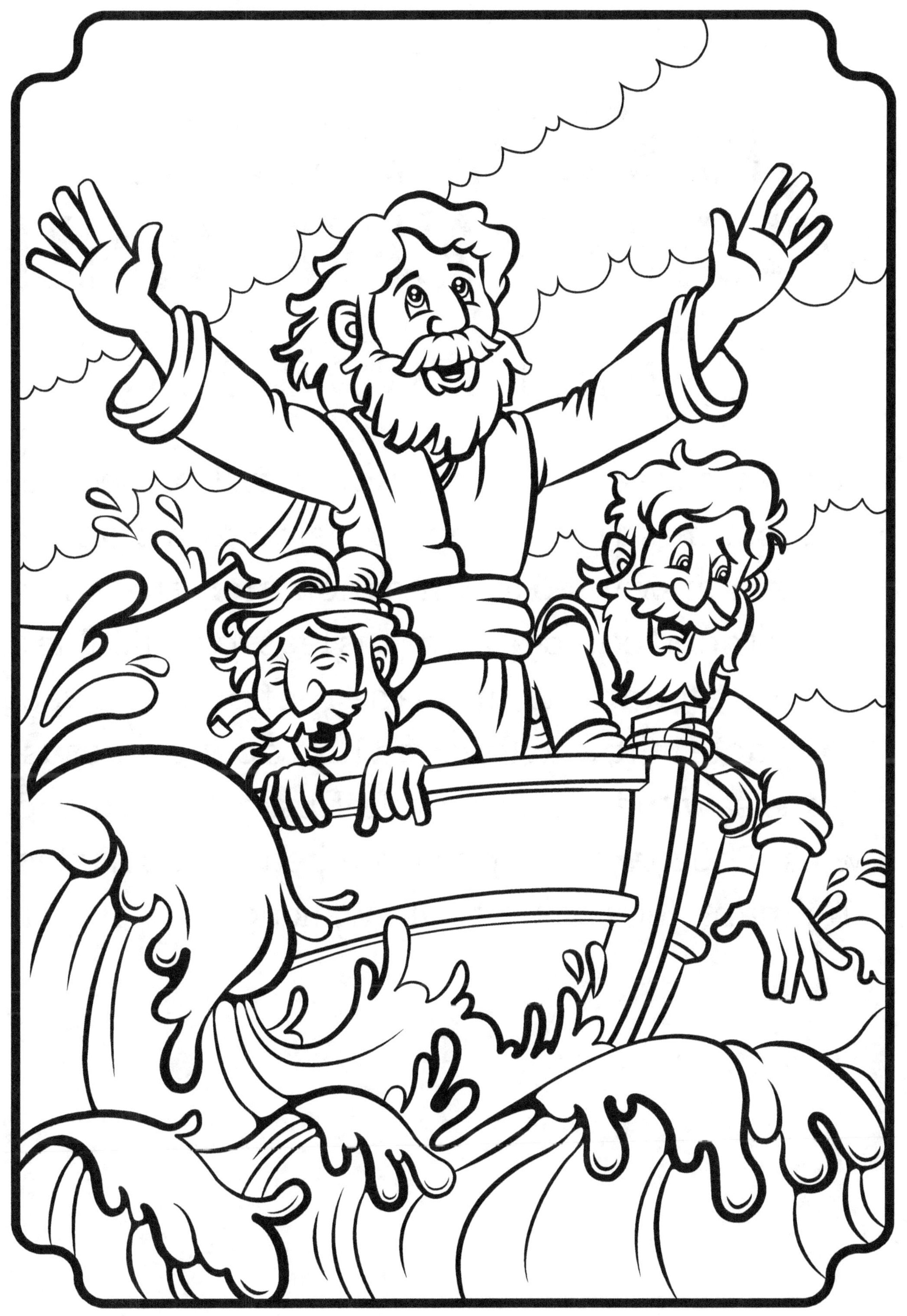

# JESUS HEALS PARALYZED MAN

## MATTHEW 9:2-8

Jesus was teaching in a house full of people. There were so many people inside, and outside! Some men wanted to bring their friend to Jesus. Their friend could not use his legs to walk! They carried their friend up to the roof of the house, cut a hole in it, and lowered him down to Jesus. Jesus saw the man and told him to get up and walk. The man got up and walked! Jesus healed the man's legs so he could walk again!

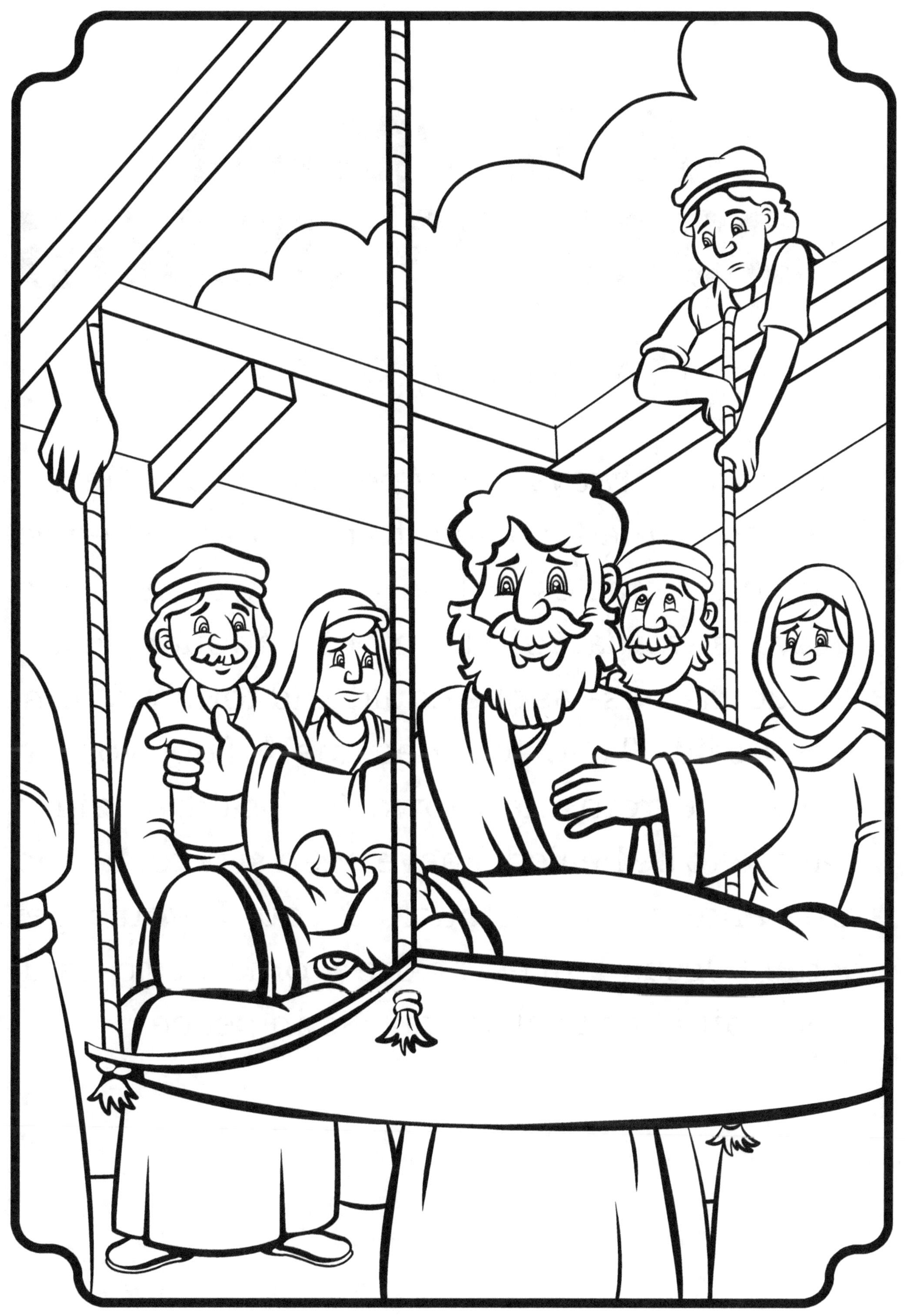

# A WOMAN TOUCHES JESUS

## MATTHEW 9:20-22

There were always many people around Jesus. They all wanted to listen to him and be healed with his miracles. While Jesus was in a big crowd, a woman tried her best to touch Jesus. She got as close as she could and touched him. Jesus said, "Who touched me?" The woman came out from the crowd and said, "I did. I wanted to be healed. I have been sick for a long time and knew if I touched you, I would get better." Jesus smiled at the woman and said, "Your faith has healed you. Go in peace."

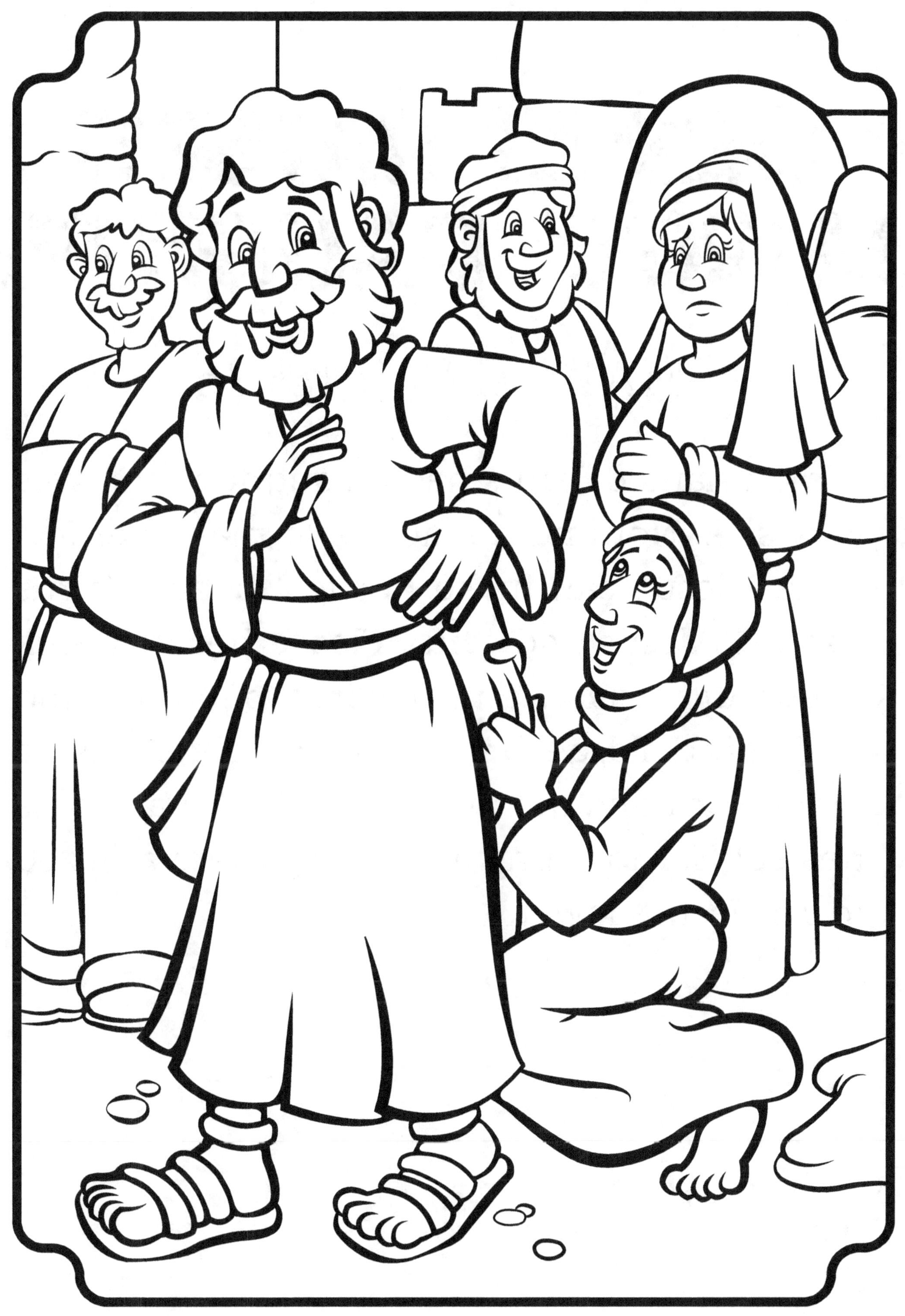

# JESUS RAISES JAIRUS' DAUGHTER

## MATTHEW 9:18-26

A man named Jairus had a daughter who was very sick. Nothing he did could make her feel better. Jesus can make her feel better! Jairus came to Jesus and said, "Please heal my sick daughter." Jesus went to Jairus' daughter and said, "My child, get up!" Jairus' daughter was no longer sick and got up! She felt better and was healed! Her mommy and daddy were amazed to see Jesus' power.

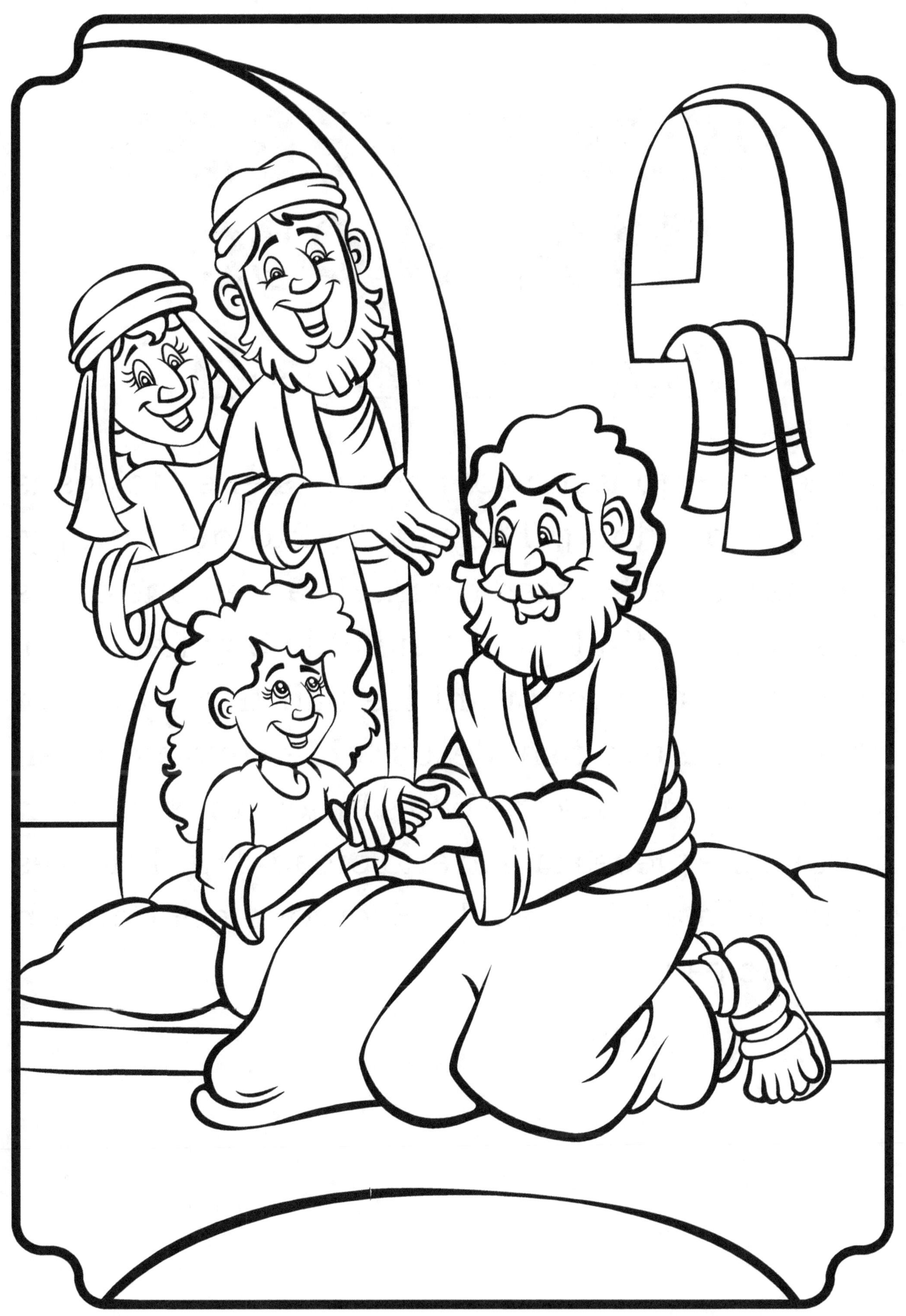

# JESUS FEEDS THE 5,000

## MATTHEW 14:13-21

One day, thousands of people listened to Jesus talk all day long! They started to get hungry. Jesus wanted to feed them. He asked one of his disciples to find food. One little boy had food, but it was not enough! He had five loaves of bread and two fish. Jesus told everyone to sit down. Jesus took the boy's lunch, prayed, then broke the pieces of fish and bread. The disciples gave it to all the people. Everyone got enough food to eat!

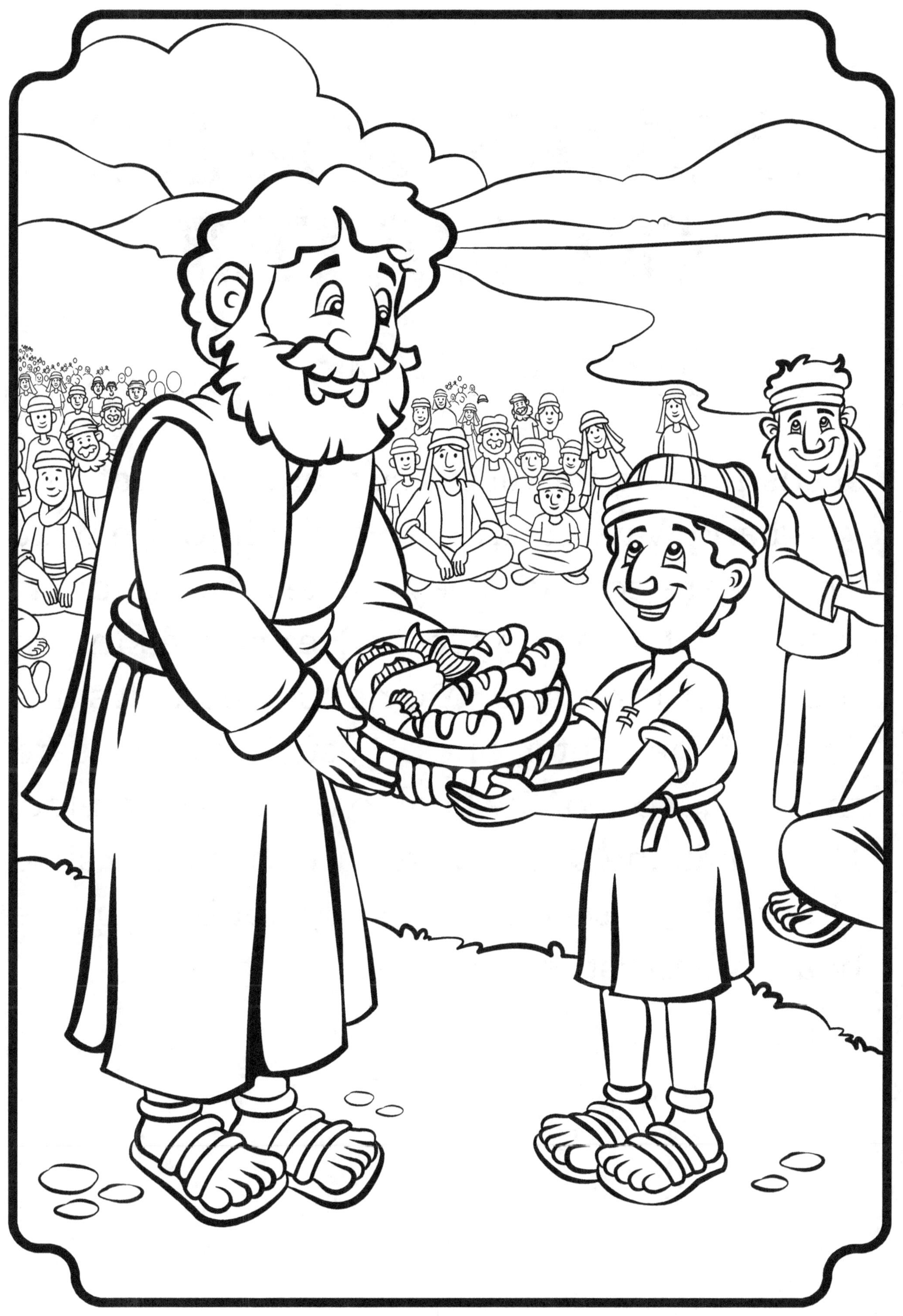

# JESUS WALKS ON WATER

## MATTHEW 14:22-33

Jesus' helpers, the disciples, were on a boat. The wind and waves started to crash into the boat. They were scared! They looked out into the stormy water and saw Jesus! He was walking on the water! Jesus said, "Do not be afraid! It's me, Jesus!" When Peter, one of Jesus' helpers heard this, he got out of the boat to walk on water too. He saw all the scary waves and began to sink. Oh no! Jesus saved him. They got back in the boat, and the storm stopped.

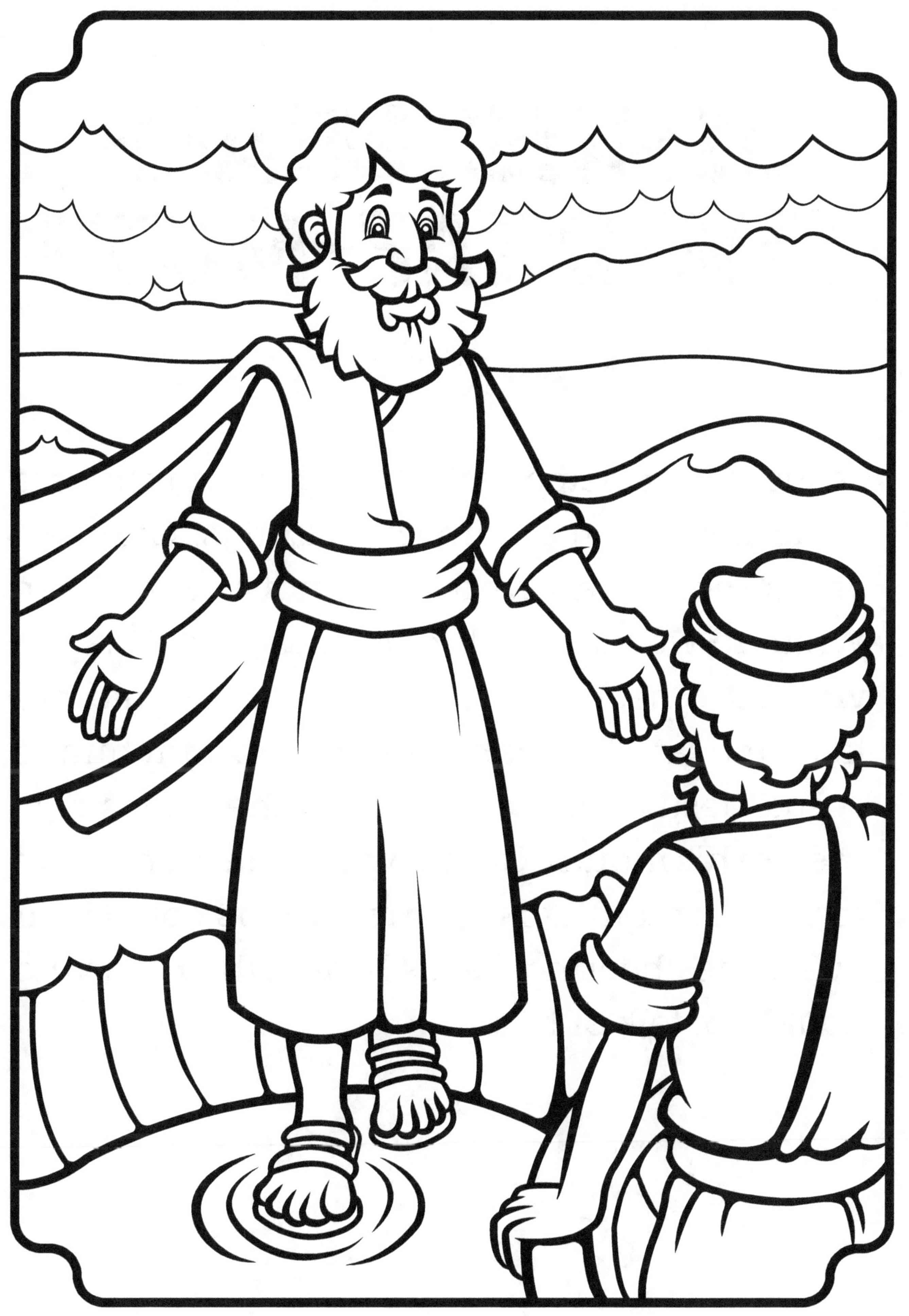

# JESUS HEALS THE DEAF-MUTE

## MARK 7:31-37

Jesus is our helper and friend. He takes care of us. Jesus can do amazing things! One day, Jesus met a man who could not talk, or hear. What do we use to talk? Our mouths! What do we use to hear? Our ears! The man could not talk, or hear. The man's friends brought him to Jesus. Jesus put his fingers in the man's ears then in his mouth. Guess what? The man began to use his mouth to talk and his ears could hear everyone cheering! Jesus healed the man who could not talk or hear.

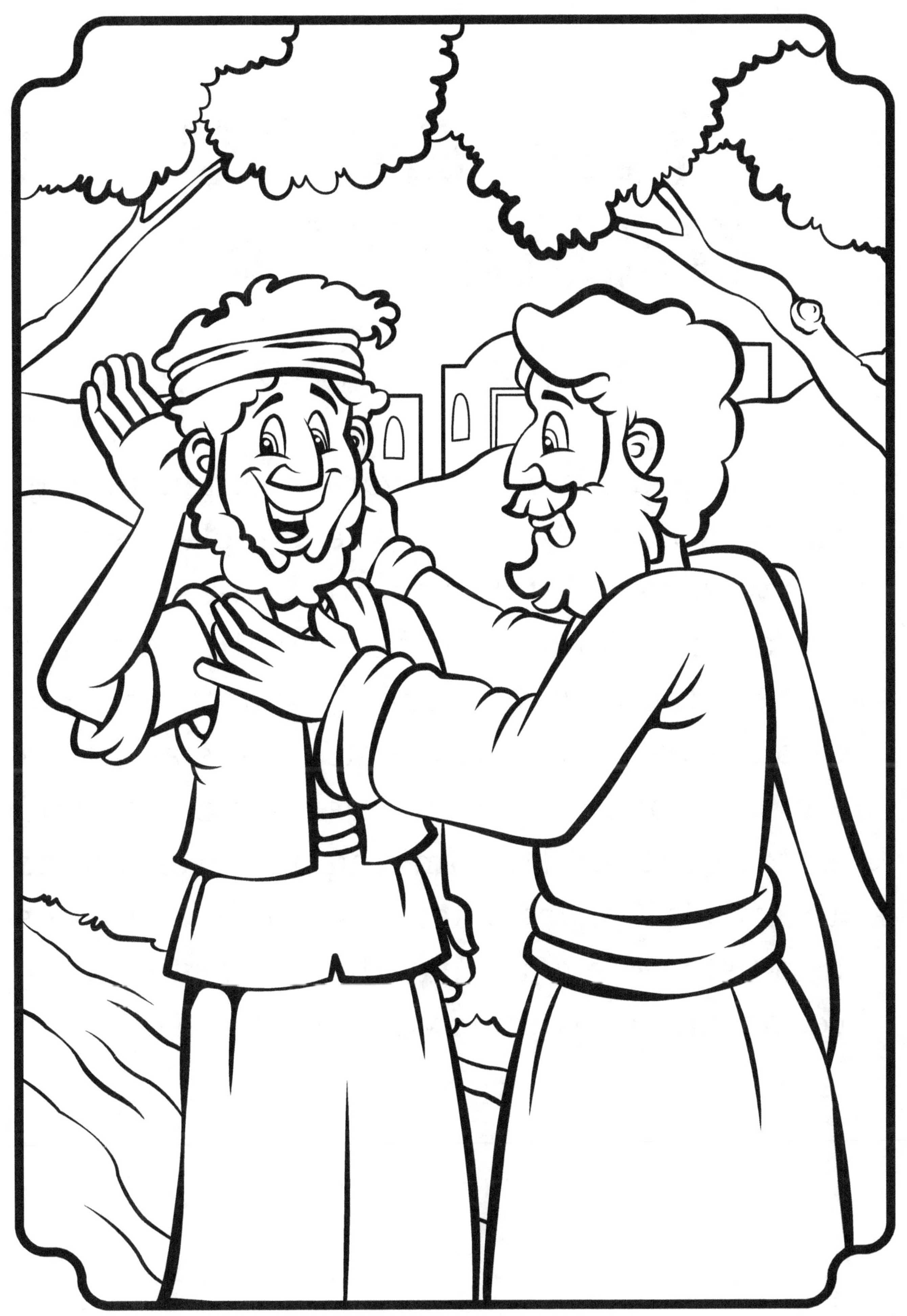

# THE GOOD SAMARITAN

## LUKE 10:25-37

Jesus helped others and wanted others to help too. One day Jesus told the people about a man who was hurt that no one wanted to help. That's sad. A Samaritan man saw the hurt man and wanted to help him! The Samaritan put bandages over the hurt man's sores and took him to an inn so he could get some food and rest to get better. The Samaritan man saved the hurt man's life! Jesus tells us that he wants us all to help others just like the Samaritan man. We too can help others when they are hurt.

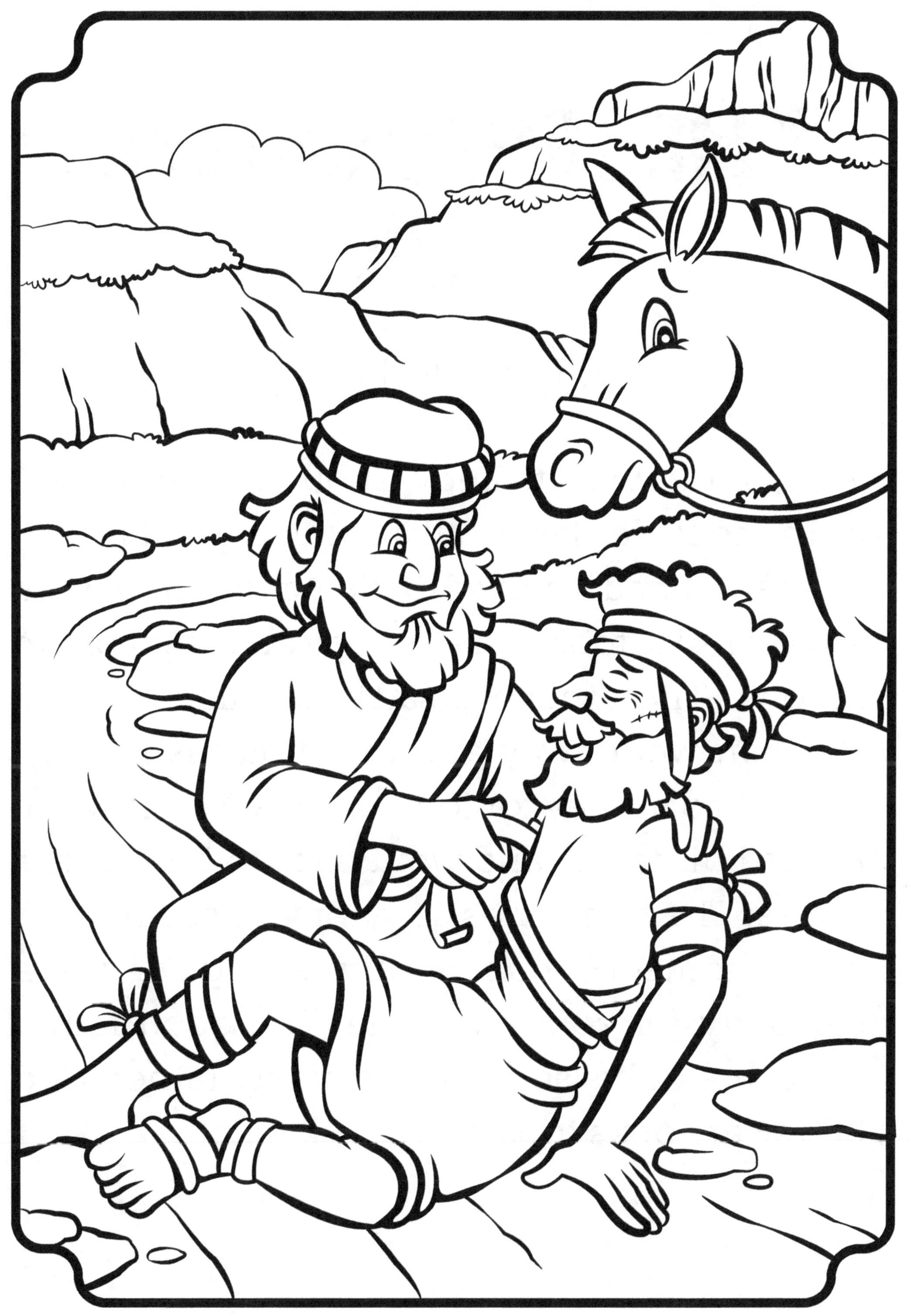

# THE PRODIGAL SON

## LUKE 15:11-32

Jesus wants us all to know about how good God is. In the Bible, Jesus talks about a good father. The father had a son who did not want to work anymore. He took some money and went off on his own. The father was sad to see his son leave. The son went away and spent all his money. He had no money for food or a place to stay. He missed his father and went back to his father's house. The father was so happy to see his son come home! He hugged him and gave him a big party for coming home. The good father took care of his son. Our heavenly father, God takes care of us too.

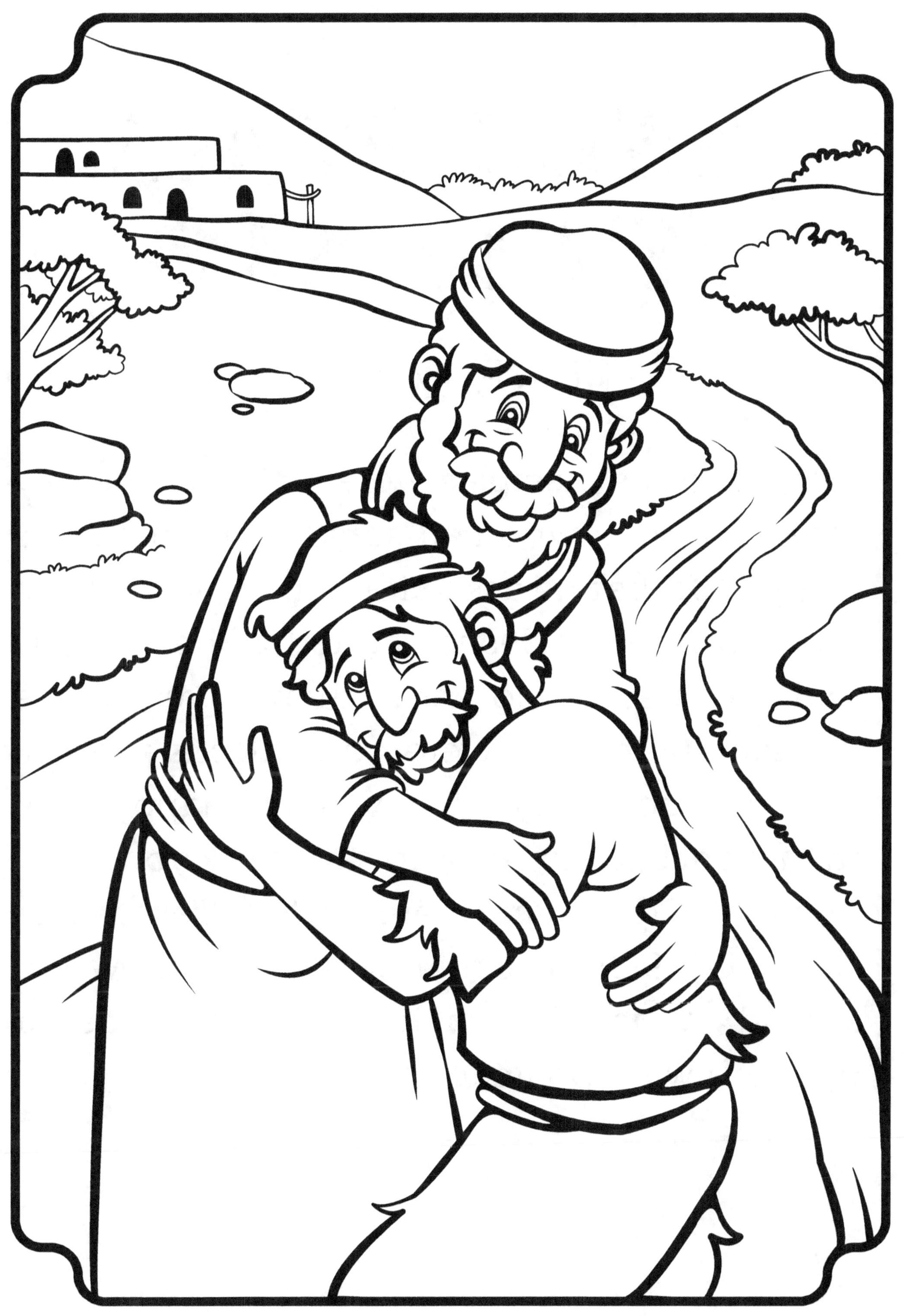

# JESUS HEALS TEN LEPERS

## LUKE 17:11-19

Jesus and his disciples were walking one day when ten men who had sores on their bodies stopped Jesus and asked for help. They were so sad and hurting. Jesus wanted to help. Jesus told the men to go show themselves to the priests. Their sores were gone! Jesus took all the boo-boos away! They were so happy. One man went back to Jesus to say thank you. Only one man! How many were healed? Ten! 1-2-3-4-5-6-7-8-9-10! The man was thankful. We too should be thankful when others do things for us. It is always polite to say thank you!

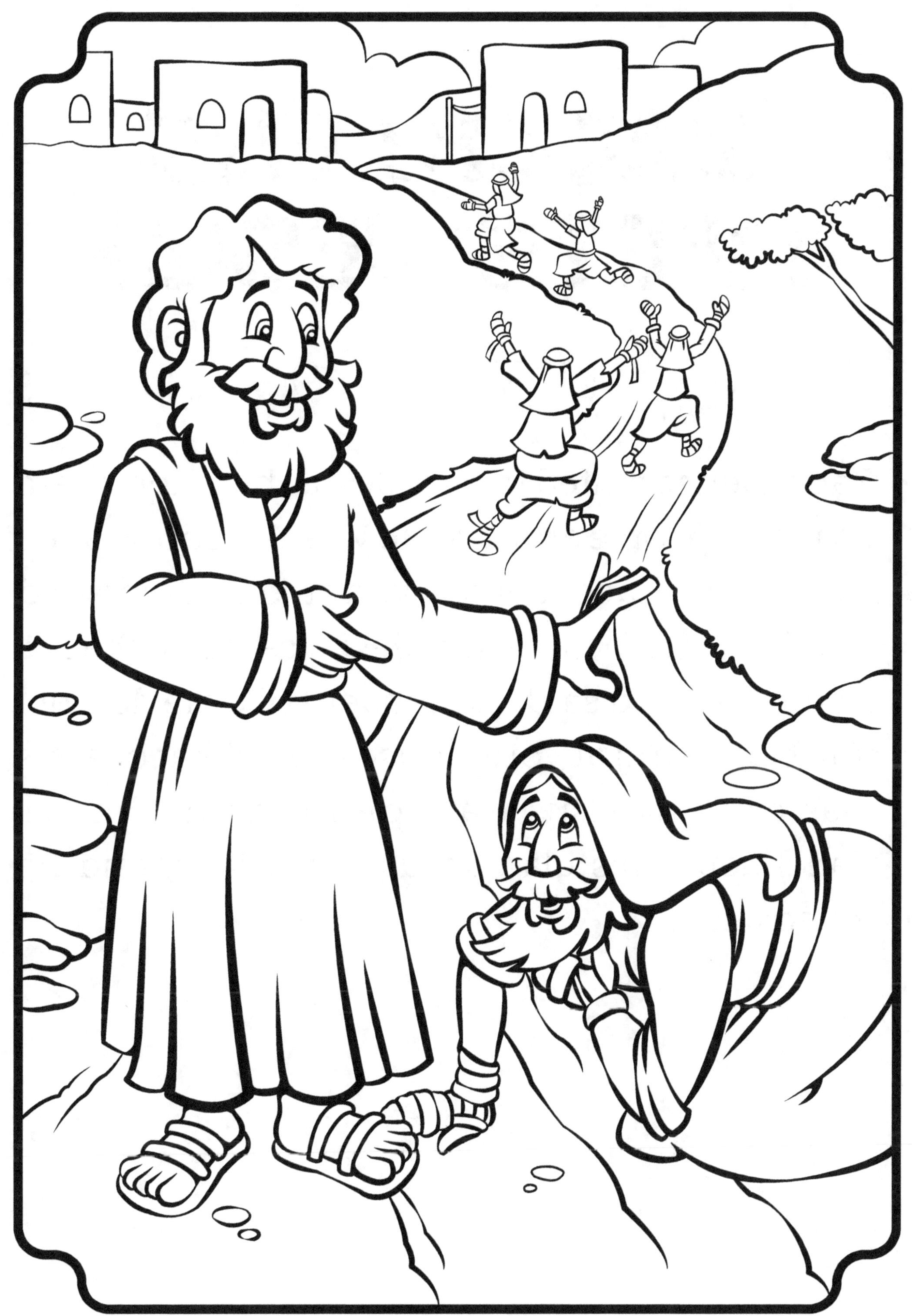

# ZACCHAEUS MEETS JESUS

## LUKE 19:1-9

Zacchaeus wanted to hear Jesus, but there were so many people around! He was too short to see over them. Zacchaeus saw a tree and decided to climb it to hear Jesus. Jesus saw Zacchaeus in the tree and said, "Zacchaeus! Come down! I will be staying at your house today!" Zacchaeus was excited! Jesus was coming to his house! Zacchaeus was glad Jesus loved him, and he loved Jesus.

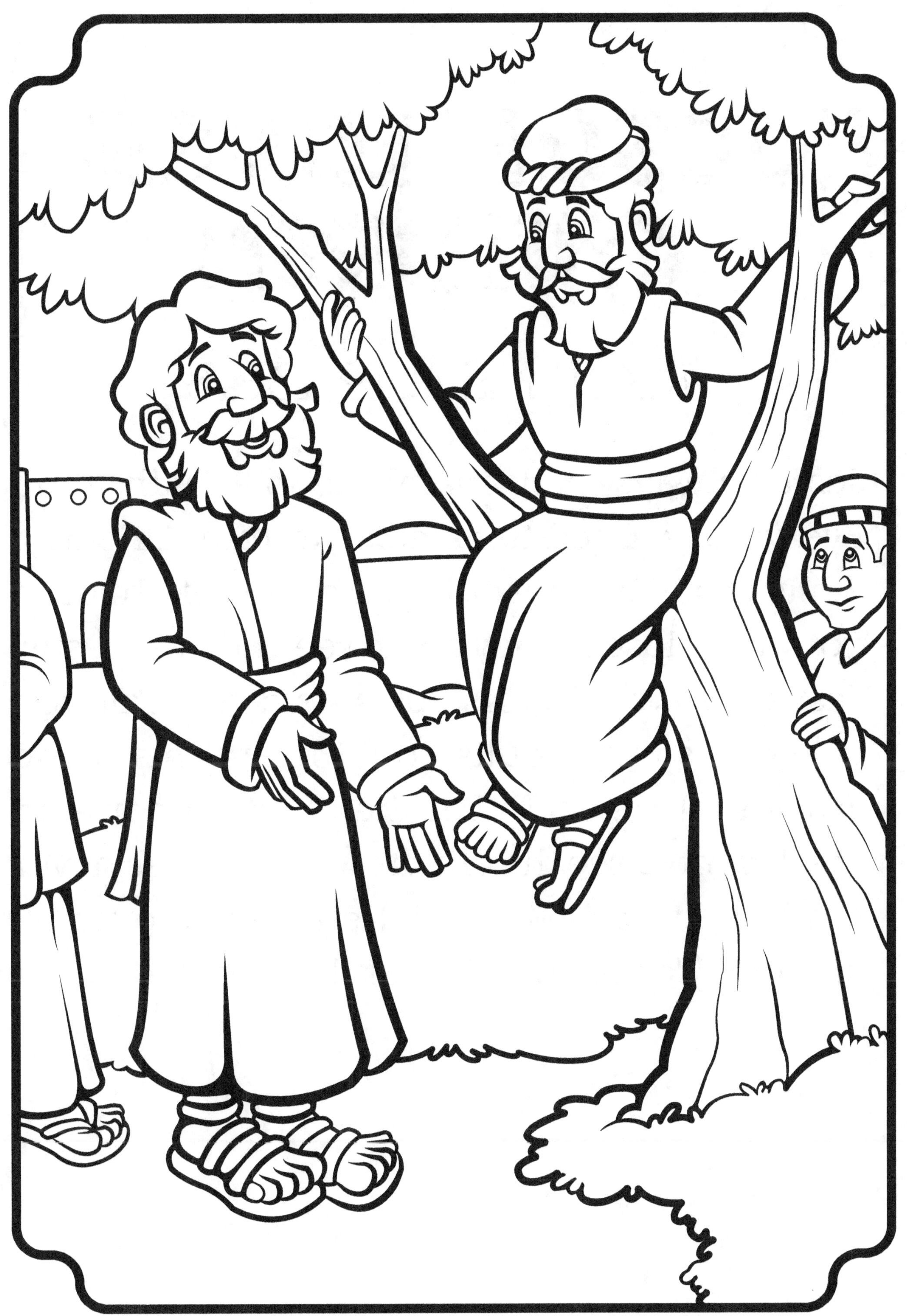

# JESUS LOVES CHILDREN

## MATTHEW 19:13-15

Jesus always had many people with him. Everyone wanted to be close to him. One day, while Jesus was teaching, a group of children got really close so they could see and hear Jesus. Jesus' helpers the disciples, told the children to move so the adults could hear. This made Jesus sad! He said, "Let the children come to me! I want to see the children!" Jesus was never too busy to sit with children. Jesus loves all children. Jesus loves you and me too!

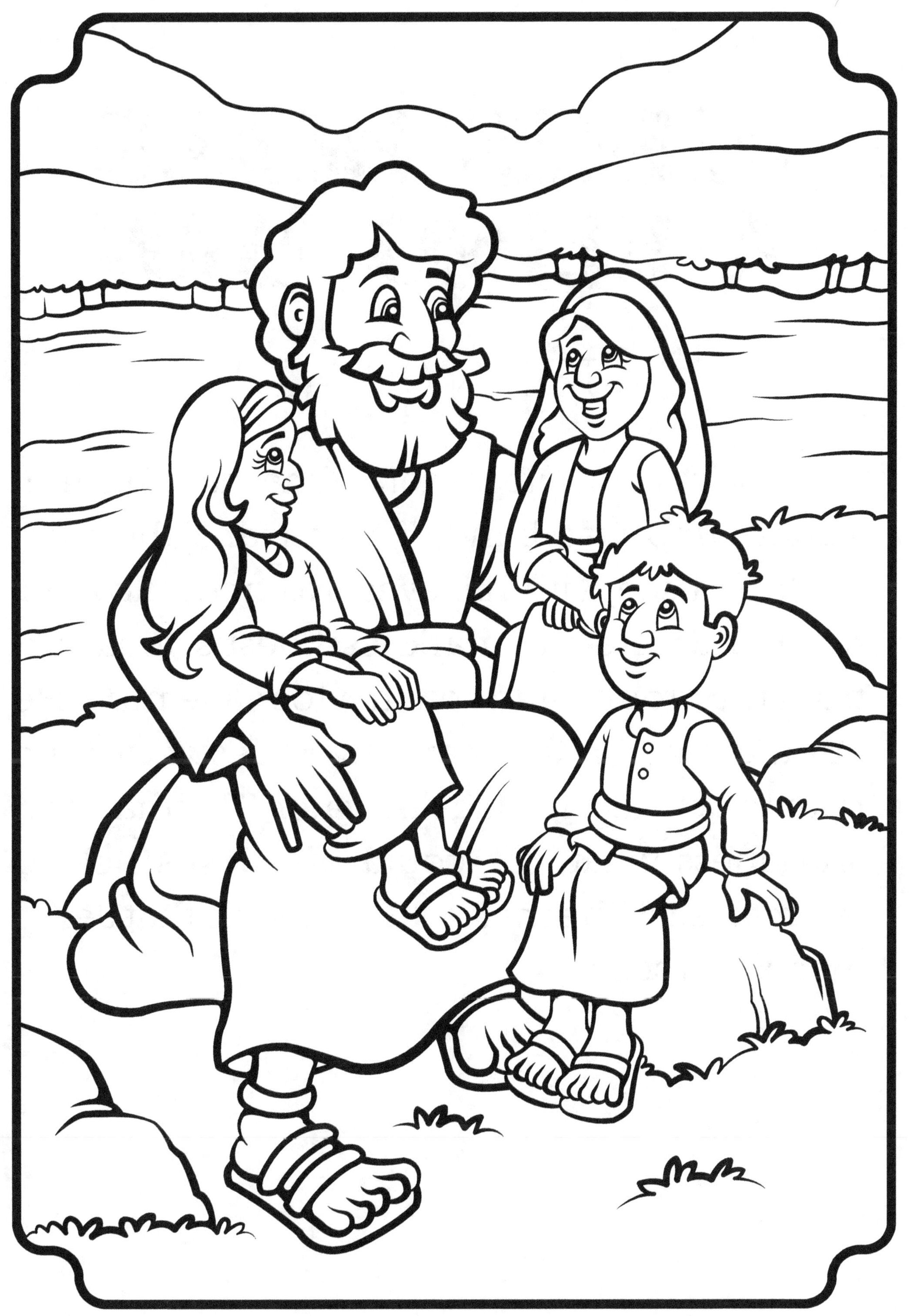

# JESUS HEALS A BLIND MAN

## JOHN 9:1-41

Jesus loves to help others. One day, he met a man who was blind. This means the man could not see with his eyes! No trees, flowers, no friends. He saw darkness! Jesus took dirt from the ground and spit in it to made mud. He put the mud on the man's eyes. Jesus told the man to go wash his face in water. The man did, and guess what? He could see! Jesus helped the man see! The man told everyone that Jesus made him see!

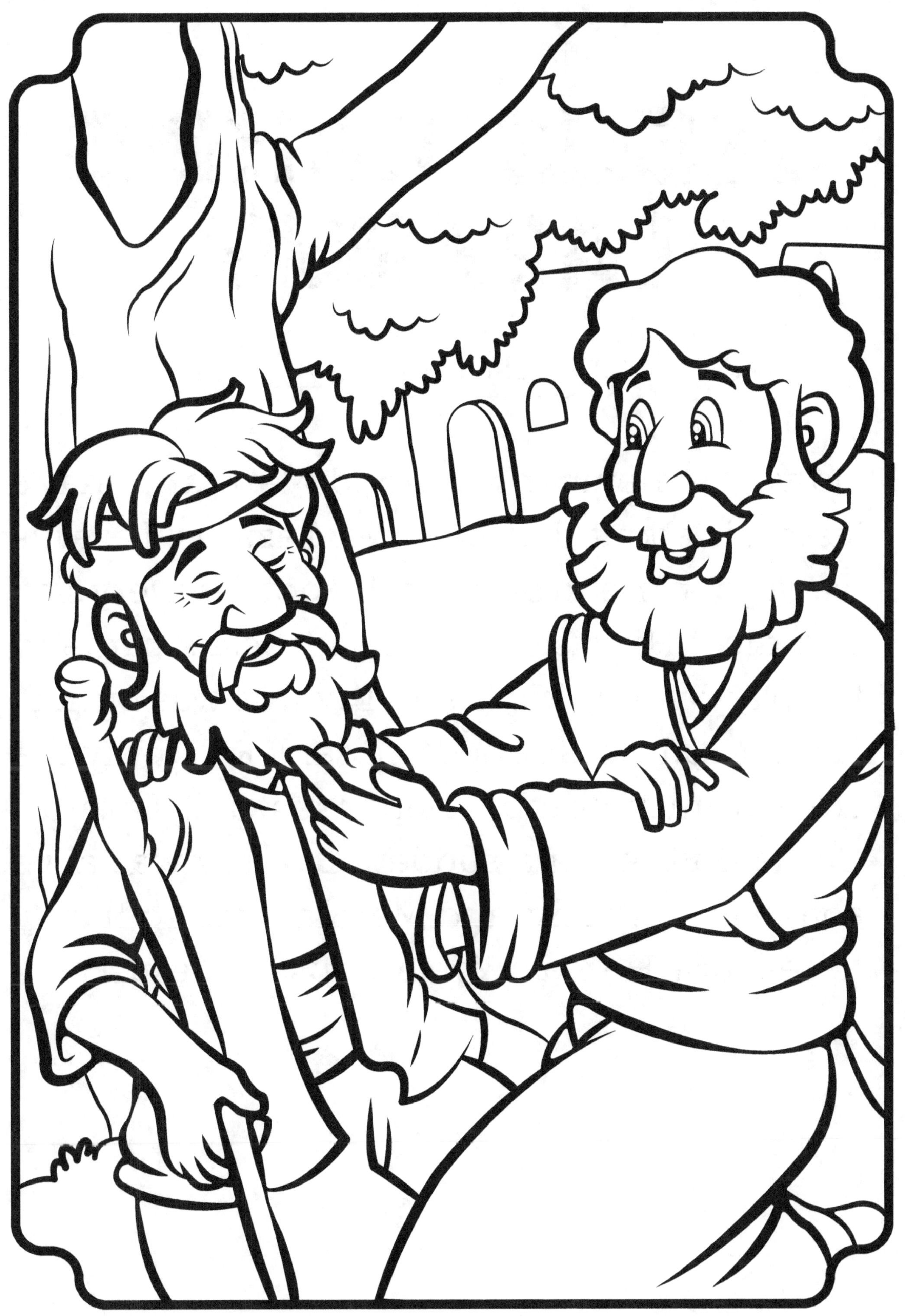

# JESUS RAISES LAZARUS

## JOHN 11:1-44

Do you remember Mary and Martha? Today's lesson is about their brother, Lazarus! Lazarus was a good friend of Jesus'. He got very very sick and died. His sisters were sad. Jesus came to the place where his friend Lazarus was buried. He was sad. Jesus cried. He said, Roll away the stone from the tomb." Then Jesus said, "Lazarus! Come out!" All of a sudden, Lazarus was alive again! Jesus, Mary, and Martha were so happy to see him. He was alive because of Jesus!

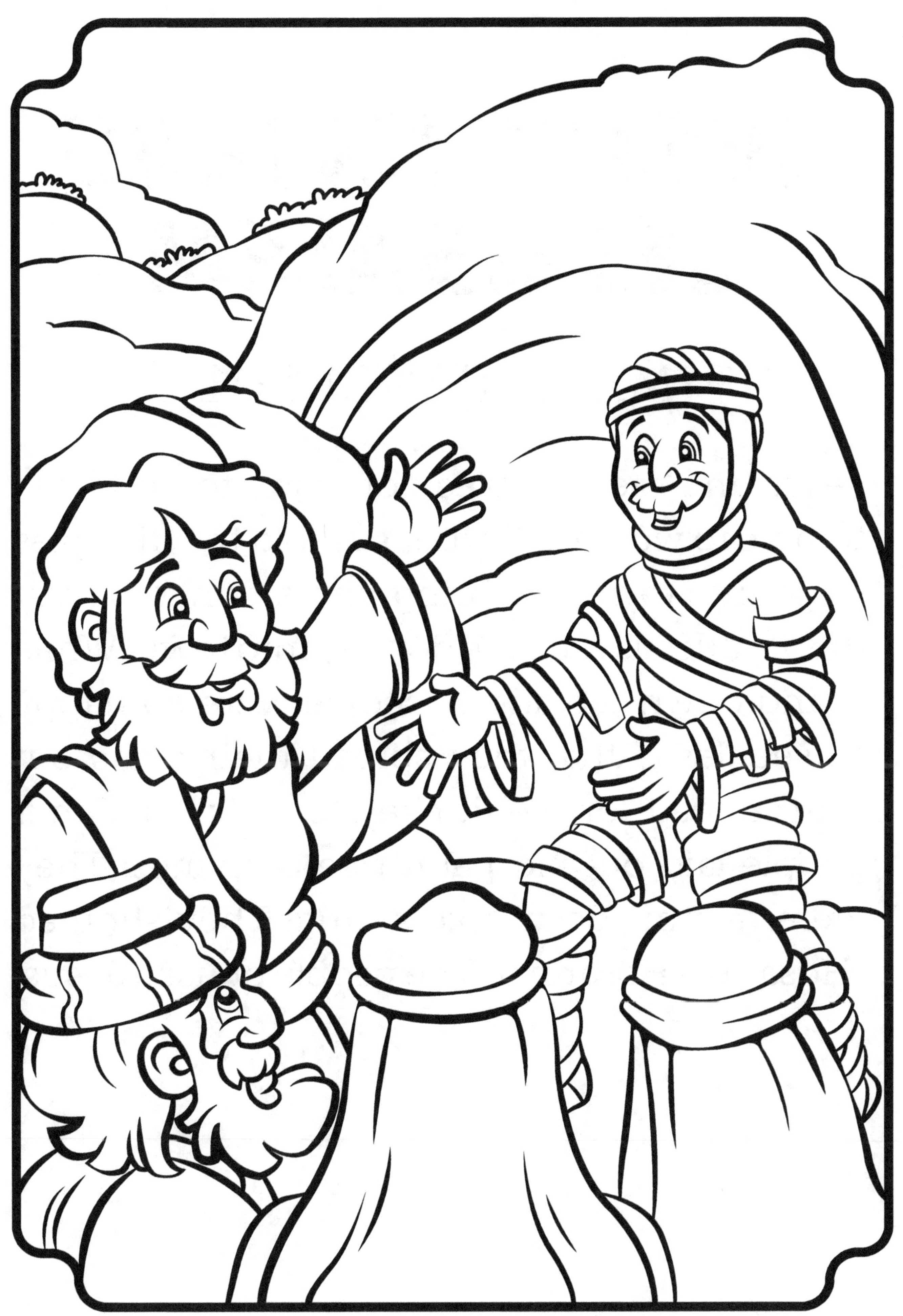

# JESUS ENTERS JERUSALEM

## MATTHEW 21:1-11

Jesus and the disciples got ready to go to the temple to worship God. Jesus told the disciples to go into town and bring him a donkey. They did, and Jesus rode the donkey into town! While going down the street, people were so happy to see Jesus that they spread their coats out on the road for the donkey to walk on! Other people laid out big palm tree branches. They were treating Jesus like a king! They shouted "Hosanna! Hosanna!" The people praised Jesus.

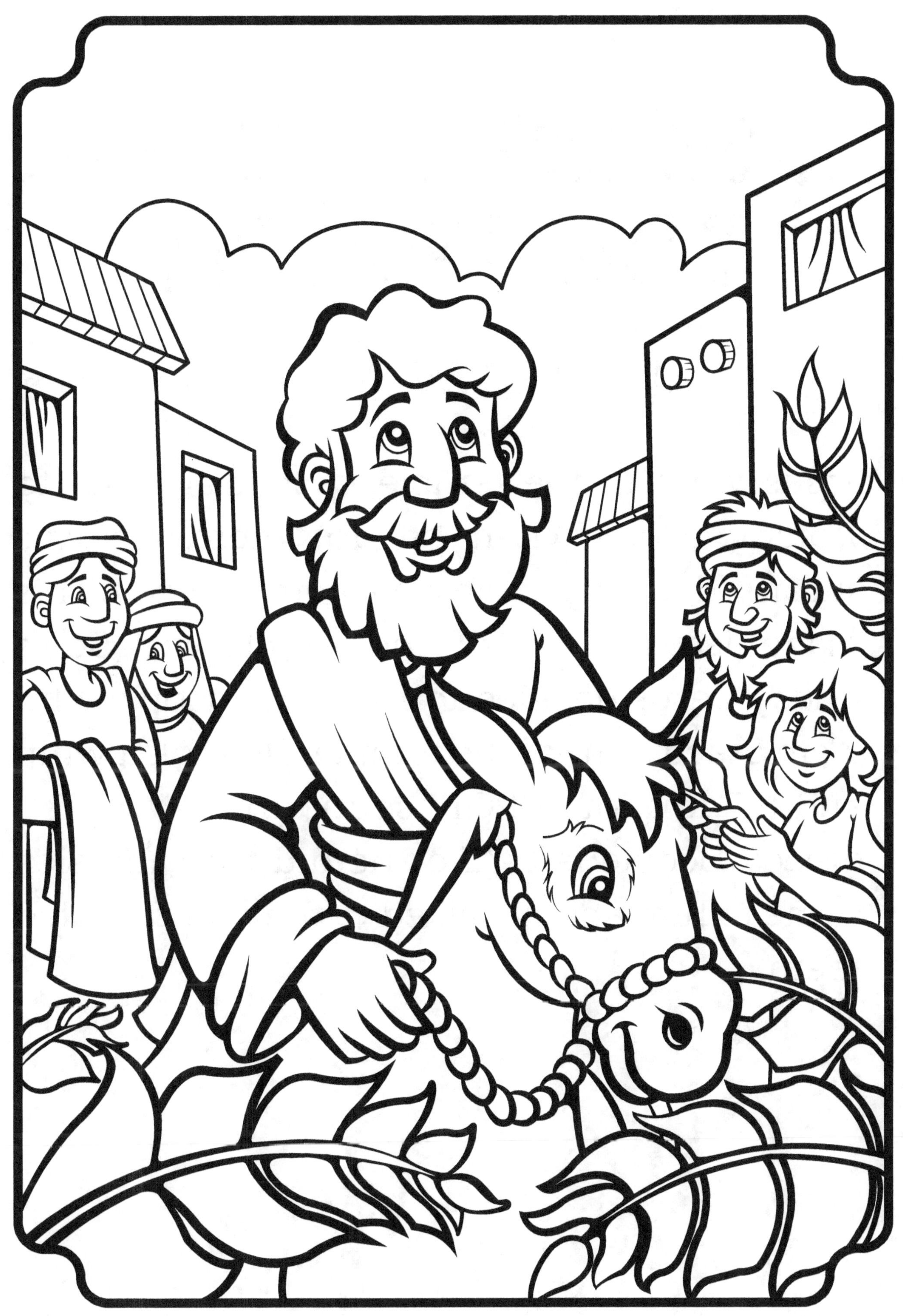

# JESUS CLEARS THE TEMPLE

## MATTHEW 21:12-16

Jesus went to the temple, a special place to worship God. When he got there, he was surprised to see people were being greedy. This made Jesus very sad. The temple was God's house! Jesus decided to force the people who were greedy out of the temple. He took a whip and made a loud "POP" sound in the air. The greedy people left. After he did this, the sick came to him and he talked to them and healed them.

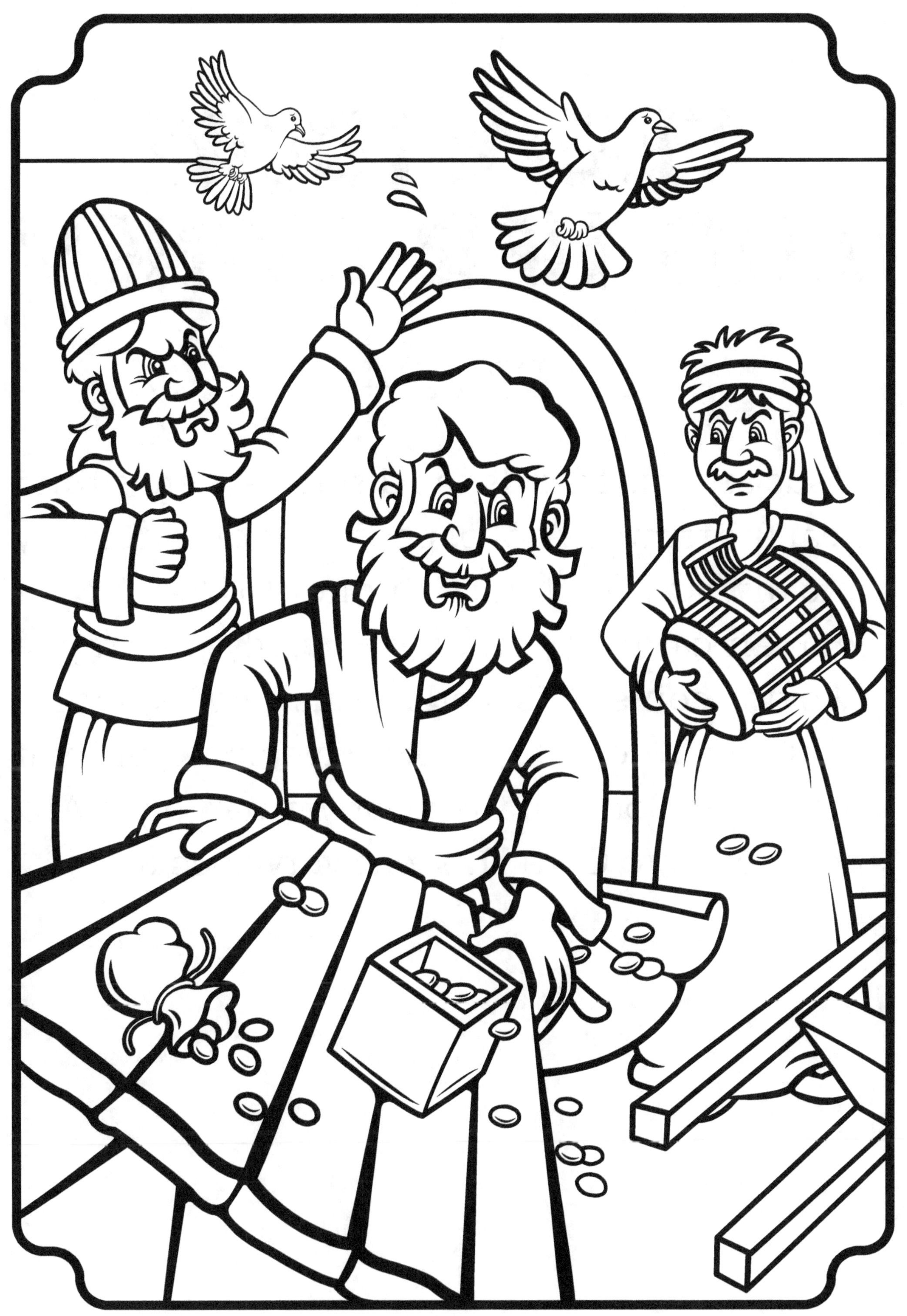

# THE WiDOW AND HER MONEY

## MARK 12:41-44

Jesus and his friends the disciples were sitting near the temple. A lot of people were coming by and giving a whole lot of money to God. A poor woman came up, and very quietly put in just two tiny coins. This made Jesus very happy. He knew that the rich people gave some of their money to God, but the poor woman gave ALL her money to God. This was very special.

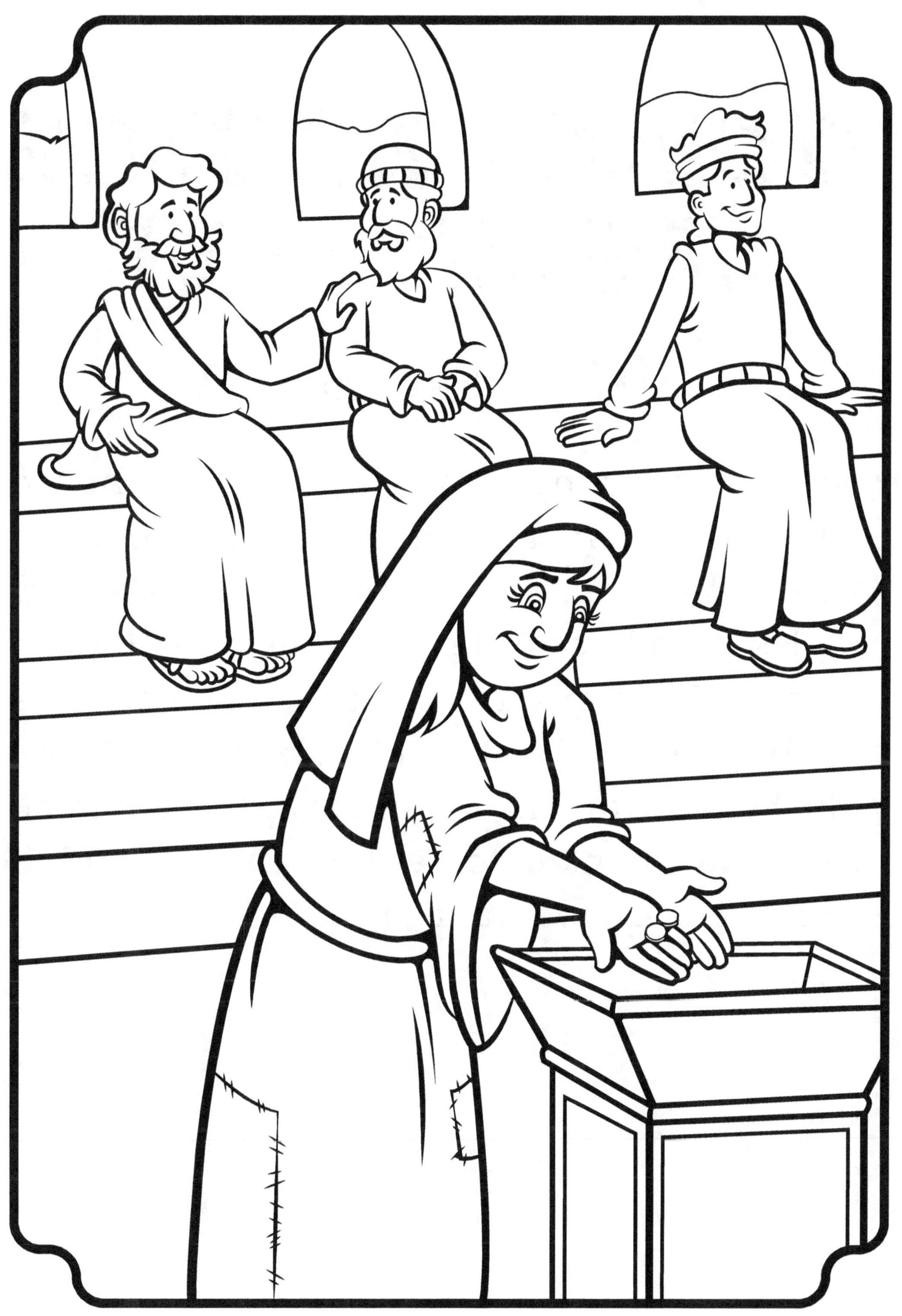

# WOMAN WASHES JESUS' FEET

## MATTHEW 26:6-13

Jesus was having dinner at a friend's house when a woman came to see Jesus. She had a very expensive jar of perfume. She walked up to Jesus and used the jar of perfume to pour all over Jesus' head and his feet. She did this to show Jesus how thankful she was for him. She bent down and began to wash Jesus' feet. Jesus was thankful to her for being so kind to him. Jesus always wants us to be kind too!

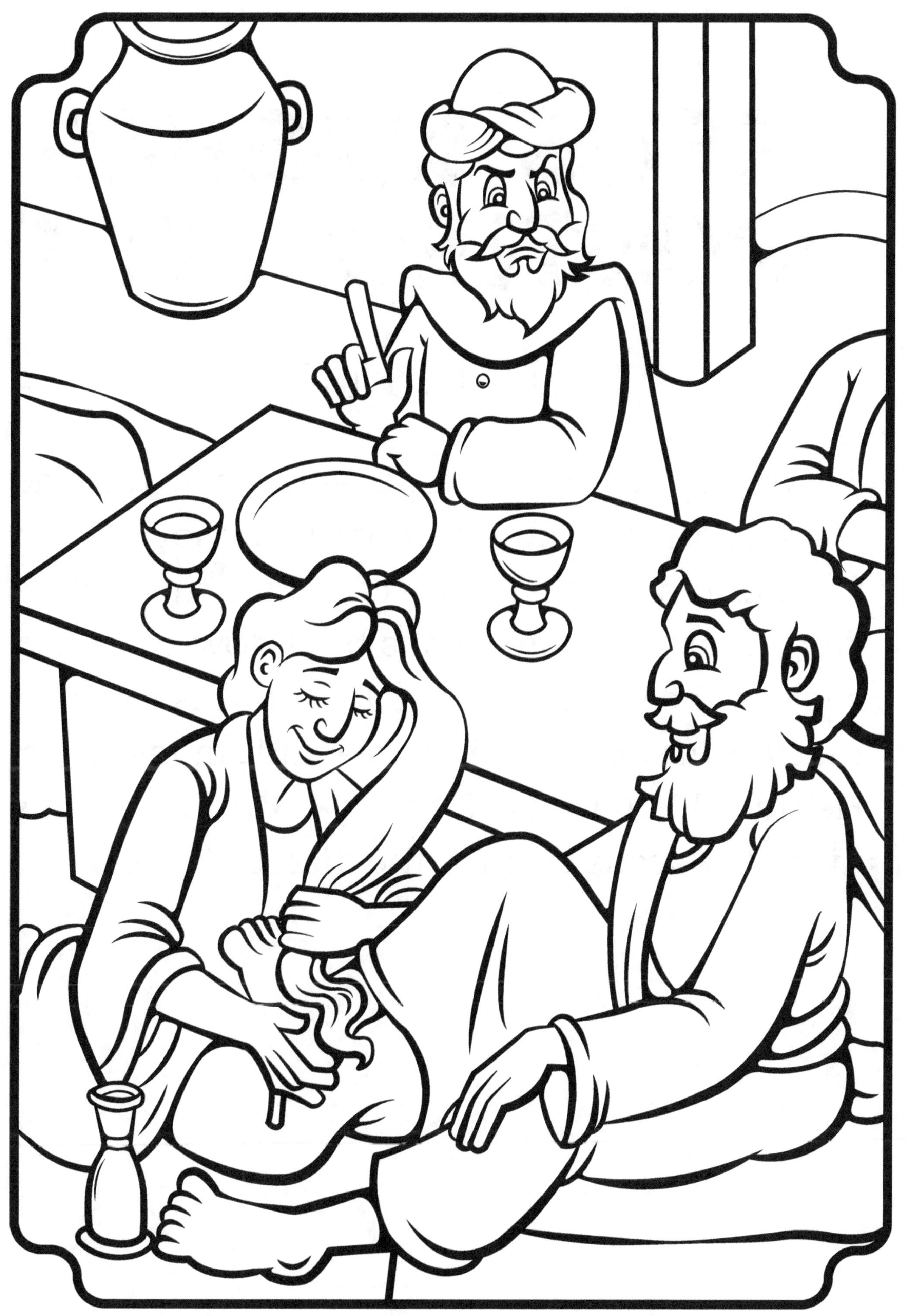

# JESUS WASHES APOSTLES' FEET

## JOHN 13:1-17

Jesus was a good friend, and he loved the disciples very much. He wanted to do something for them to show that he cared for them. One day, before they ate, Jesus bent down washed each of the disciple's feet. He did this to show that we all should be humble and serve others. He humbled himself as an example to his disciples! Jesus washed the disciple's feet.

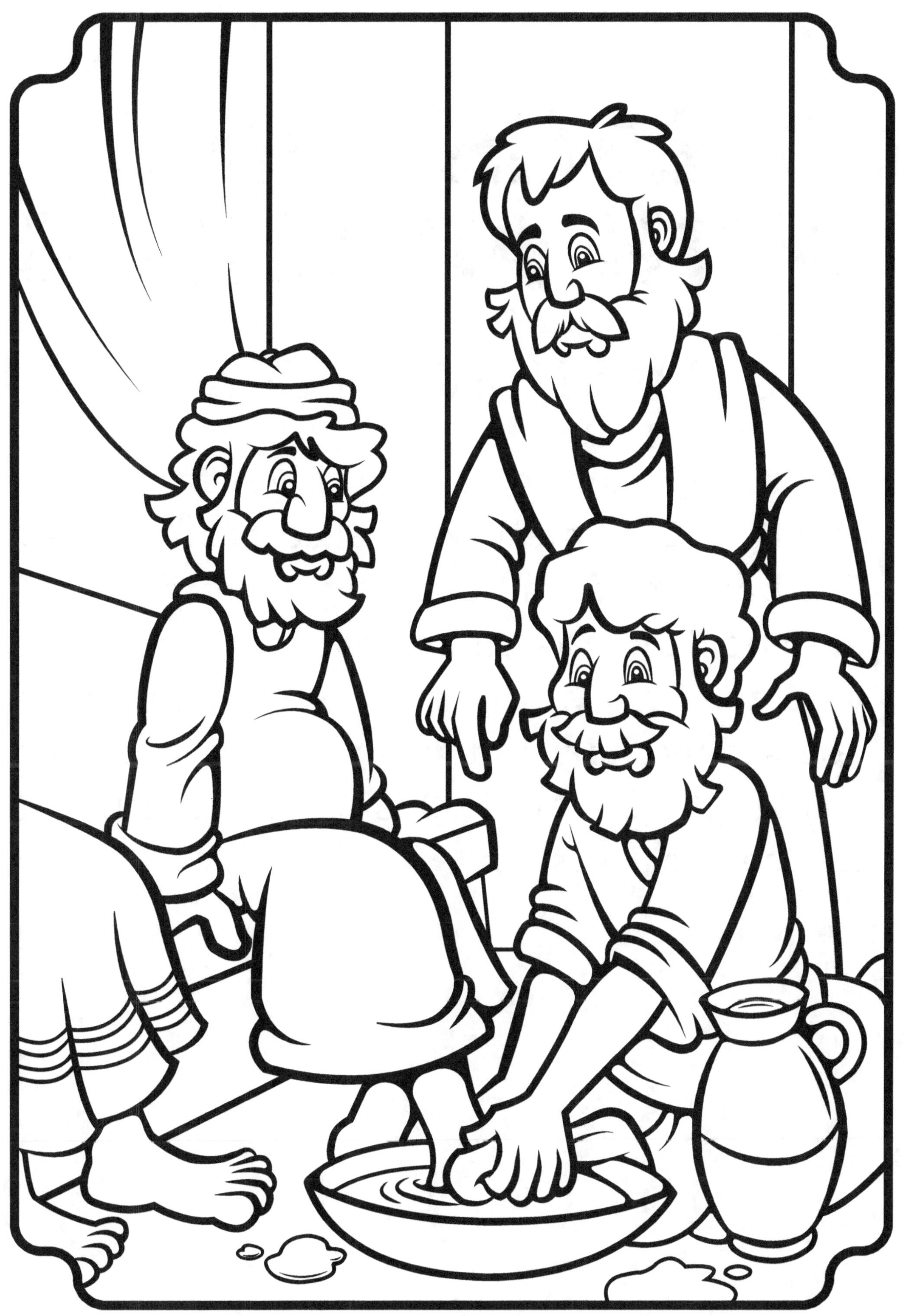

# JESUS EATS WITH APOSTLES

## MATTHEW 26:17-30

Jesus and his disciples sat down for a meal together. This meal was called the Passover. They ate bread and drank juice from grapes. Jesus told them to remember to do these things together. This is why every Sunday morning. You see mommy and daddy eating bread and drinking juice. We do this to keep our hearts focused on Jesus!

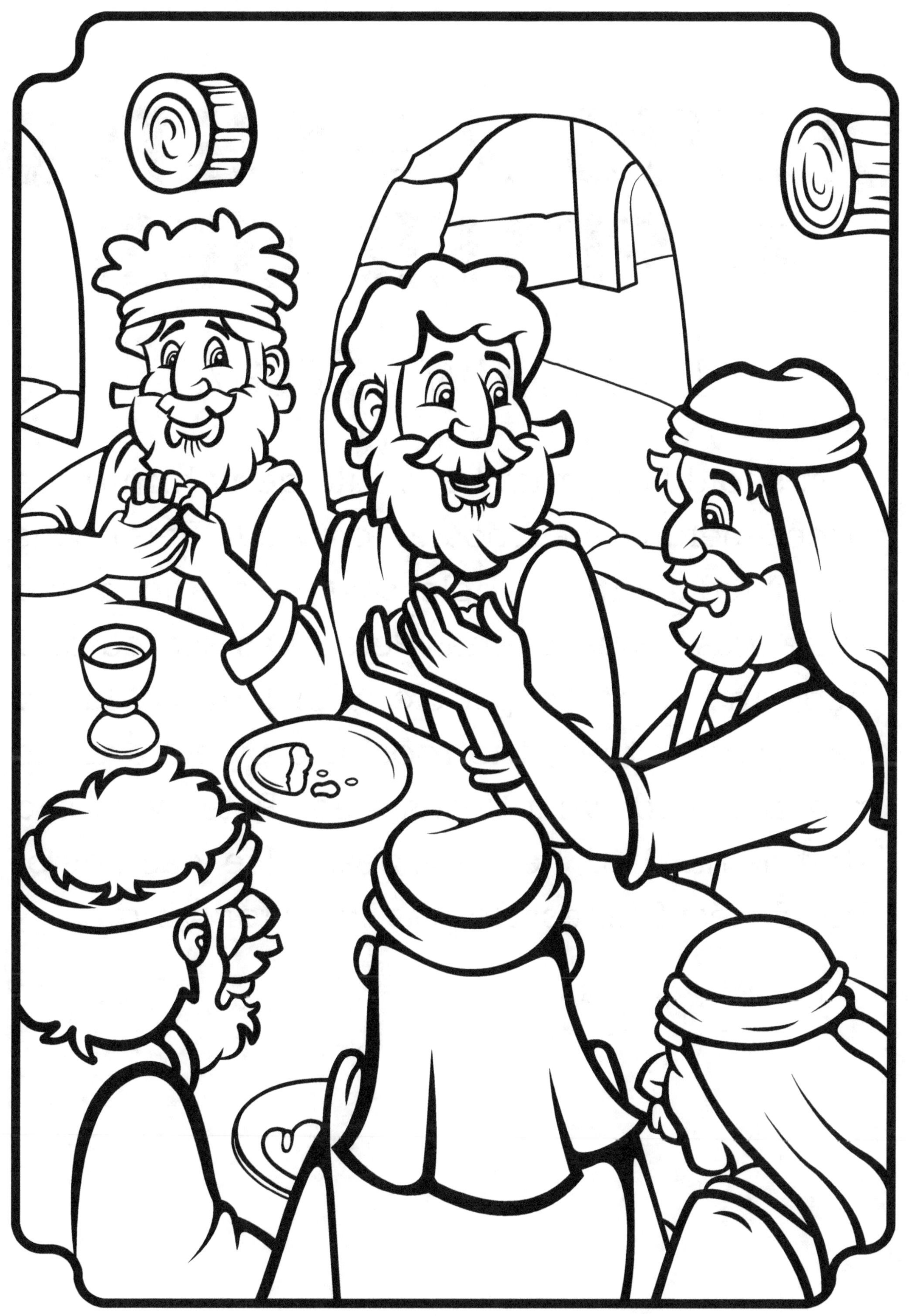

# JESUS ARRESTED & PETER LIES

## MATTHEW 26:69-75

Jesus told Peter that he would deny him three times before the rooster crowed. Peter was confused. Some people saw him and asked if he was Jesus' friend. Peter was scared and lied, and told the people "No! I didn't know Jesus!" Just then, the rooster crowed, and he remembered what Jesus said! Peter was sad that he had lied, he knew Jesus! He was one of his closest friends! He was sorry for lying.

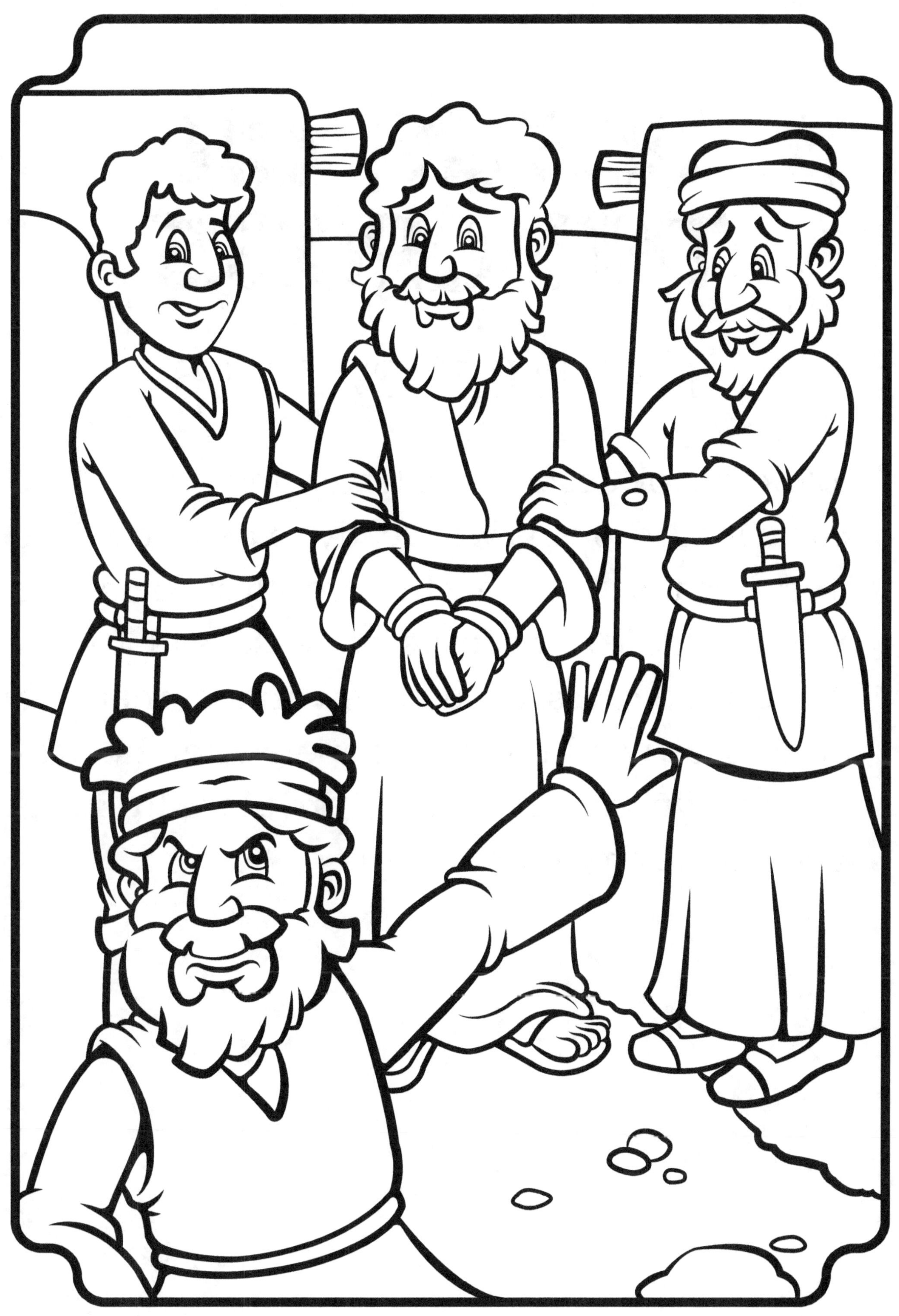

# JESUS ON THE CROSS

## MATTHEW 27:32-56

Soldiers took Jesus to be hung on a cross. This was very sad. Jesus was ready to be put on the cross because he knew this would save us. The people who loved Jesus were so sad to see him on the cross. Jesus knew that something wonderful would soon happen after he was taken down from the cross. I am thankful Jesus went to the cross for all of us.

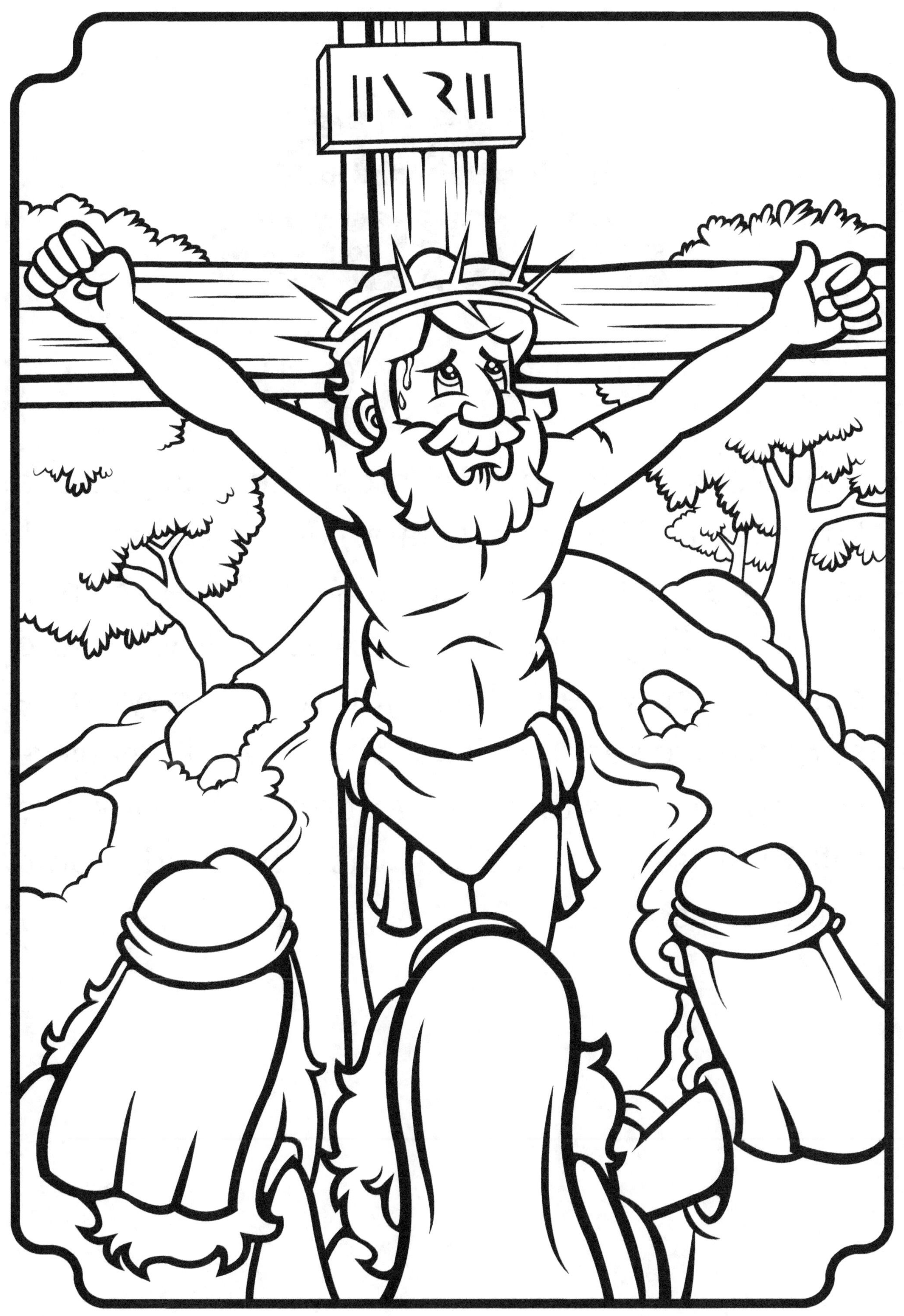
INRI

# JESUS IS RISEN

## JOHN 20:10-18

When Jesus died on the cross, he was put in a large tomb. Three days later, Jesus came back to life just like he had promised! Three women were coming to his tomb to leave flowers and spices, but when they got there they were surprised to see that Jesus was alive! They were so happy! Jesus told the women to go back and tell his disciples that he was alive and would see them soon.

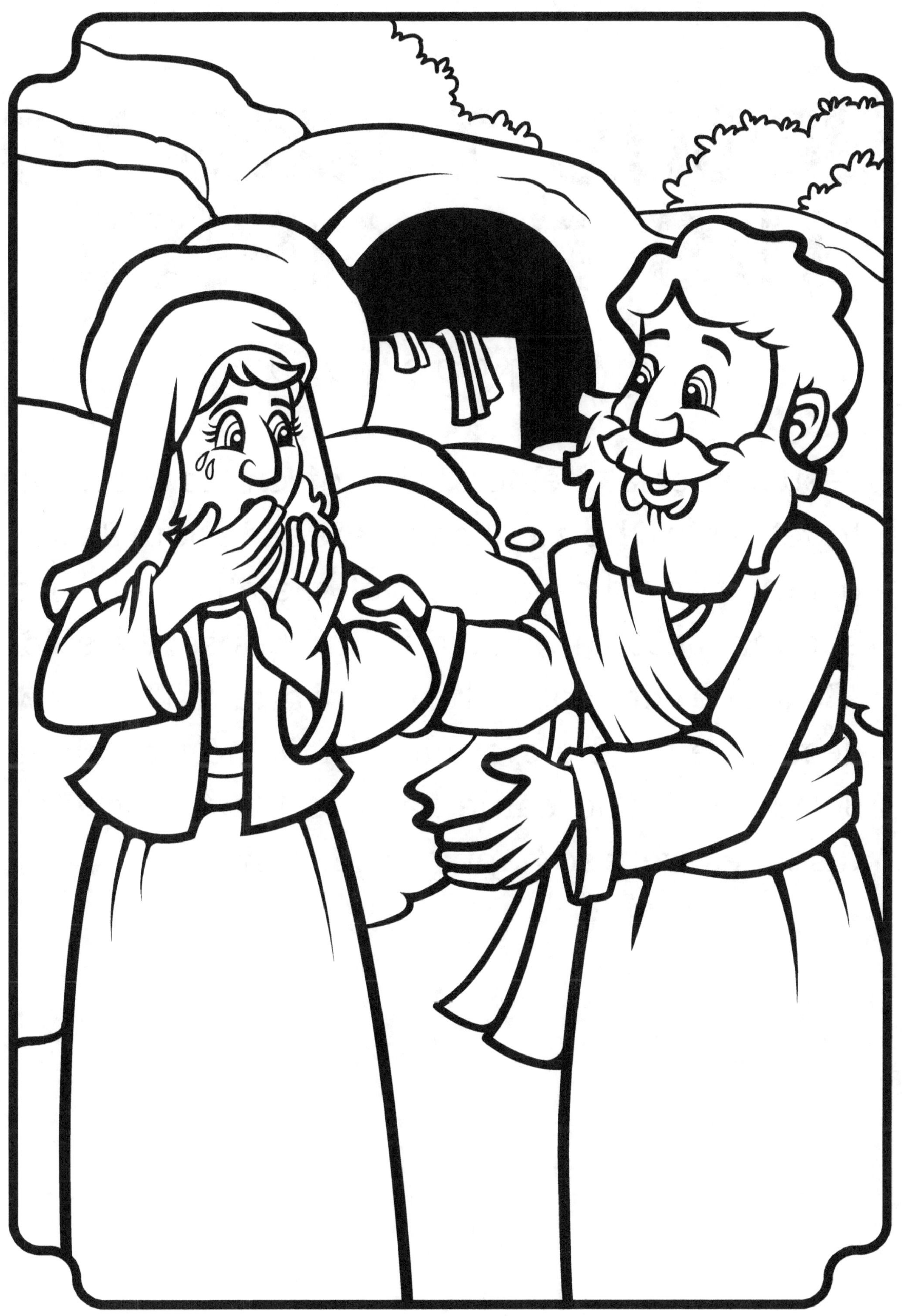

# JESUS TALKS TO HiS DiSCiPLES

## JOHN 20:19-23

Jesus' special helpers, the disciples were all together in a house. They were sad about Jesus' death. They didn't now he was alive! All of a sudden, Jesus appeared in the house! He said, "Peace be with you!" They were afraid! They saw Jesus die on the cross and now he was alive! Jesus died, and came back to life for us! The disciples were so happy to see him!

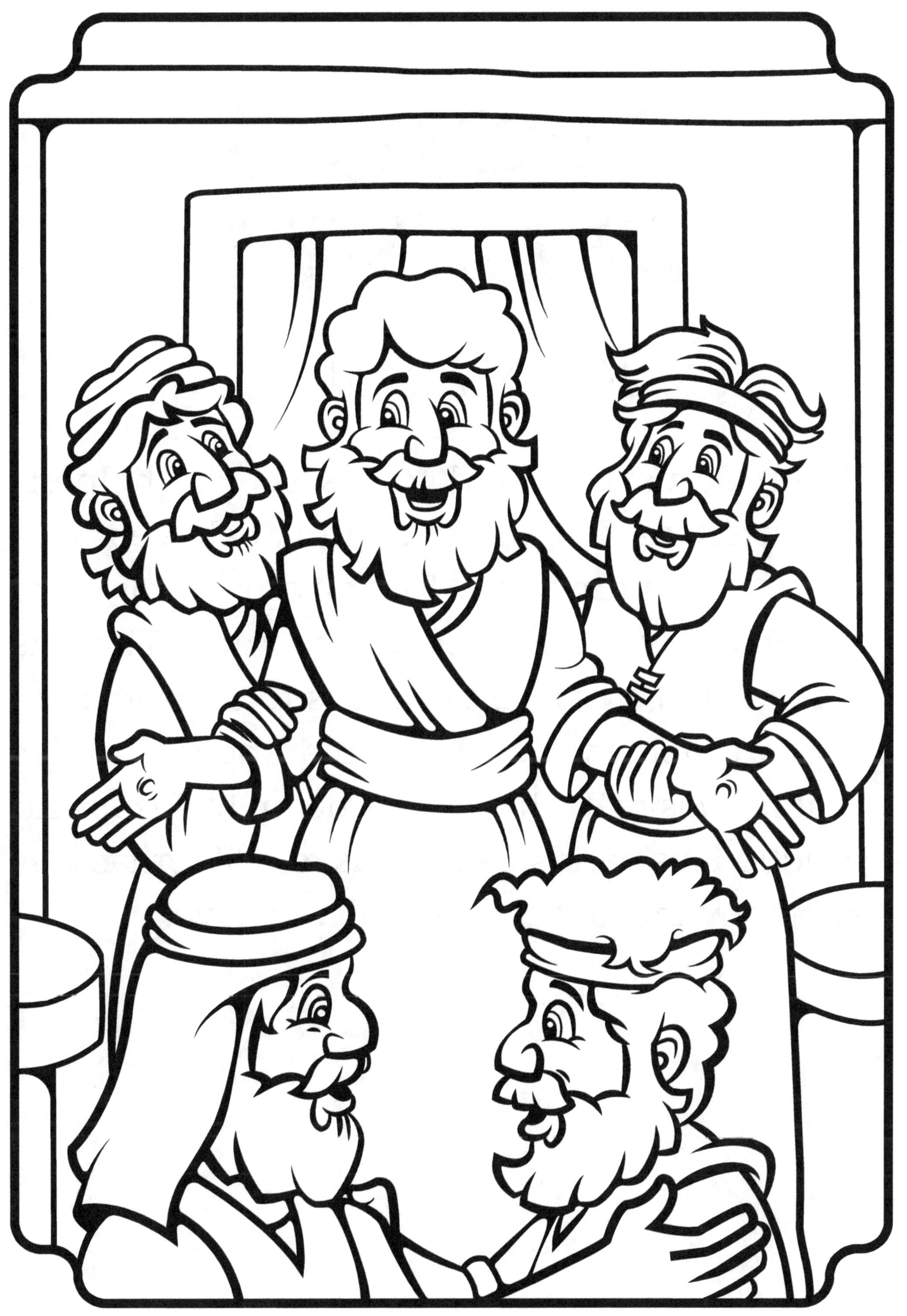

# THOMAS BELIEVES

## JOHN 20:24-29

When Jesus appeared to his special helpers, the disciples, one disciple didn't believe it was Jesus. His name was Thomas. He was very sad that Jesus had died. Jesus knew Thomas was having a hard time. Jesus told Thomas to come touch him so he could show Thomas that he was real. Thomas came up to Jesus and touched his hands. Jesus was real! Thomas was so happy that Jesus was real and alive!

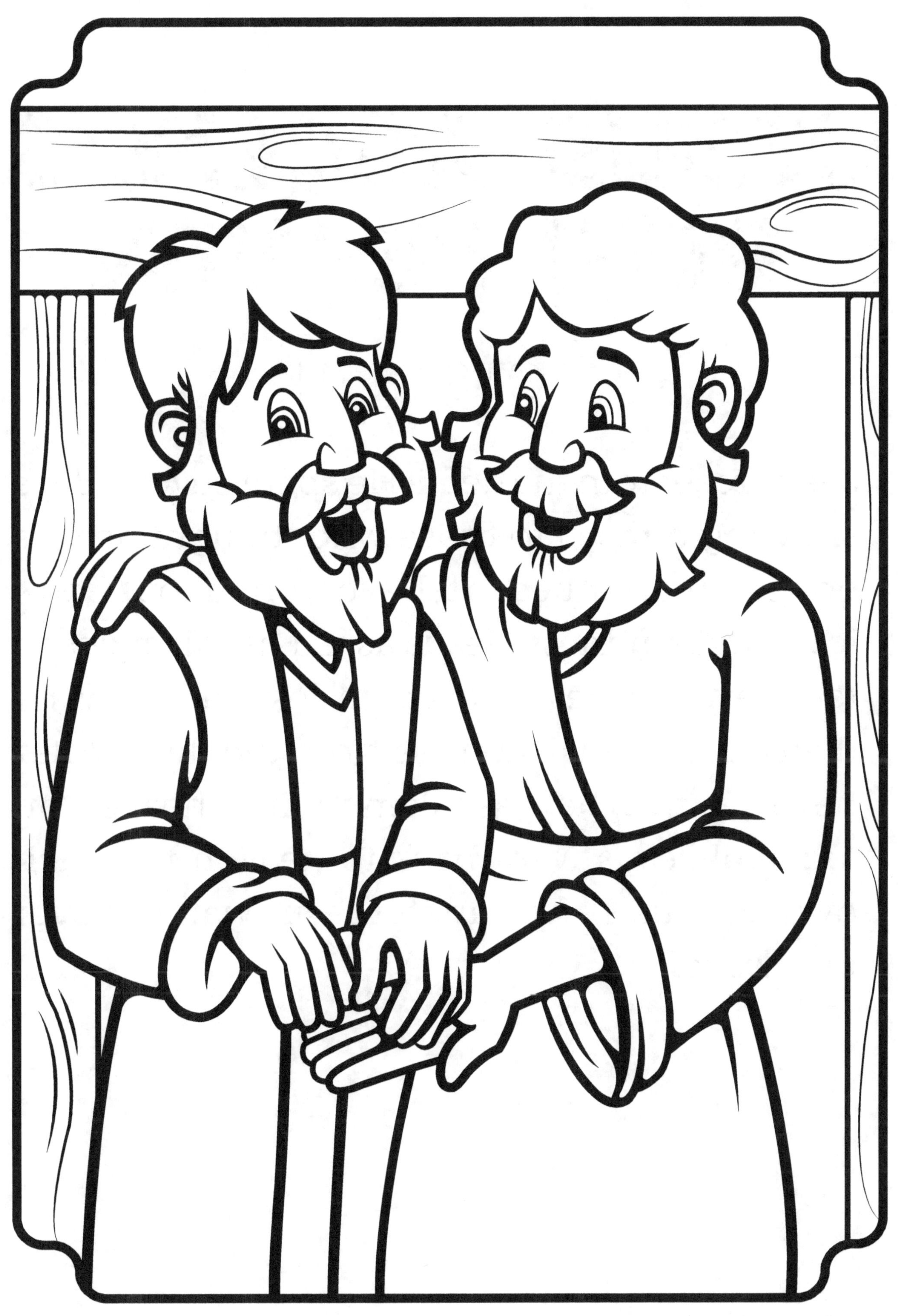

# JESUS ASCENDS INTO HEAVEN

## ACTS 1:1-11

Jesus rose from the dead! He spent several days showing himself to those who thought he was gone. He continued to tell everyone about God's love, and kindness. Jesus asked his disciples to tell everyone they meet about Jesus and how he died for our sins and rose from the dead! After he asked this, he was taken up into heaven on a cloud! Jesus went back to heaven to watch over all of us. I am thankful Jesus watches over us always!

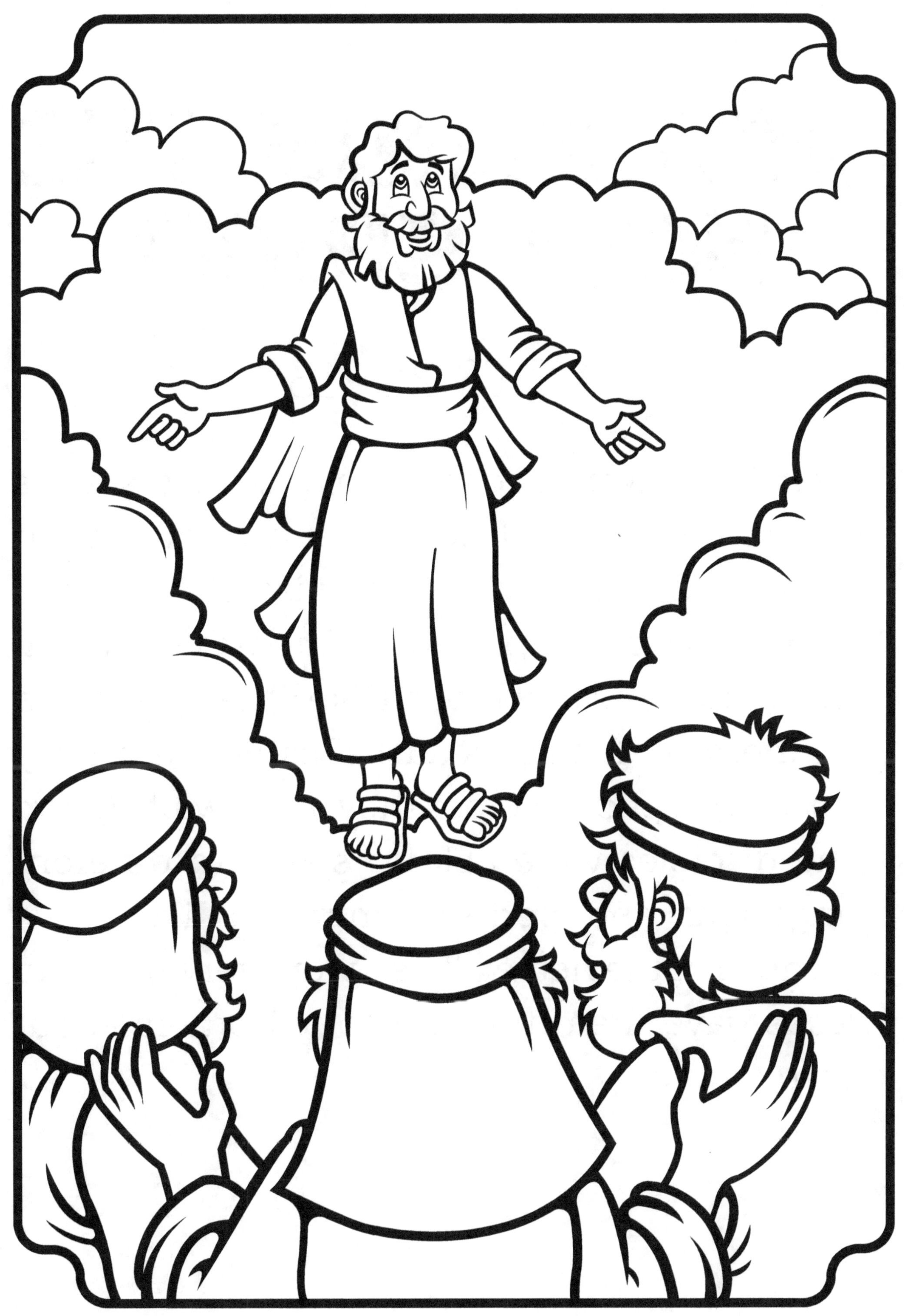

# GOD SENDS THE HOLY SPIRIT

## ACTS 2:1-13

After Jesus went back to heaven, the disciples waited for a special helper Jesus would send to them. One day, while the disciples were in a house, a strong wind blew through the room and something that looked like little fires rested on the top of their heads! This was the Holy Spirit, the special helper they were waiting for. The disciples were able to speak in different languages and perform miracles like Jesus because of the helper. They were very thankful Jesus gave them this gift to tell others about him.

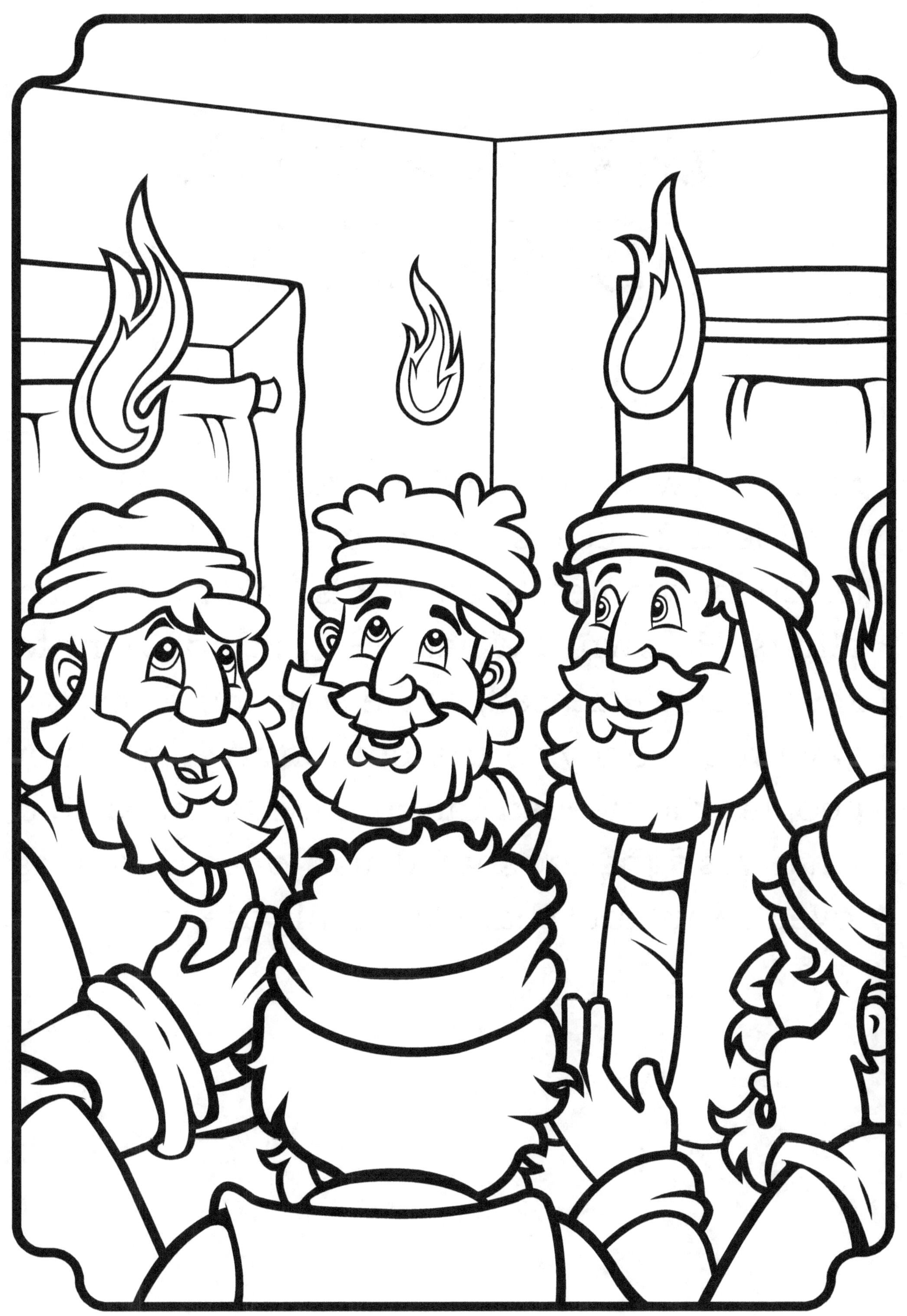

# BARNABAS SHARES

## ACTS 4:32-37

Barnabas was a man who loved Jesus. Do you love Jesus? Because Barnabas loved Jesus so much, he wanted to show his love by helping others. He owned a field. He did not want to keep it all to himself, so he sold the field, and gave the money to the church to help other people who needed the money. Barnabas did what was right, and shared his money. Barnabas loved Jesus, and shared with his friends.

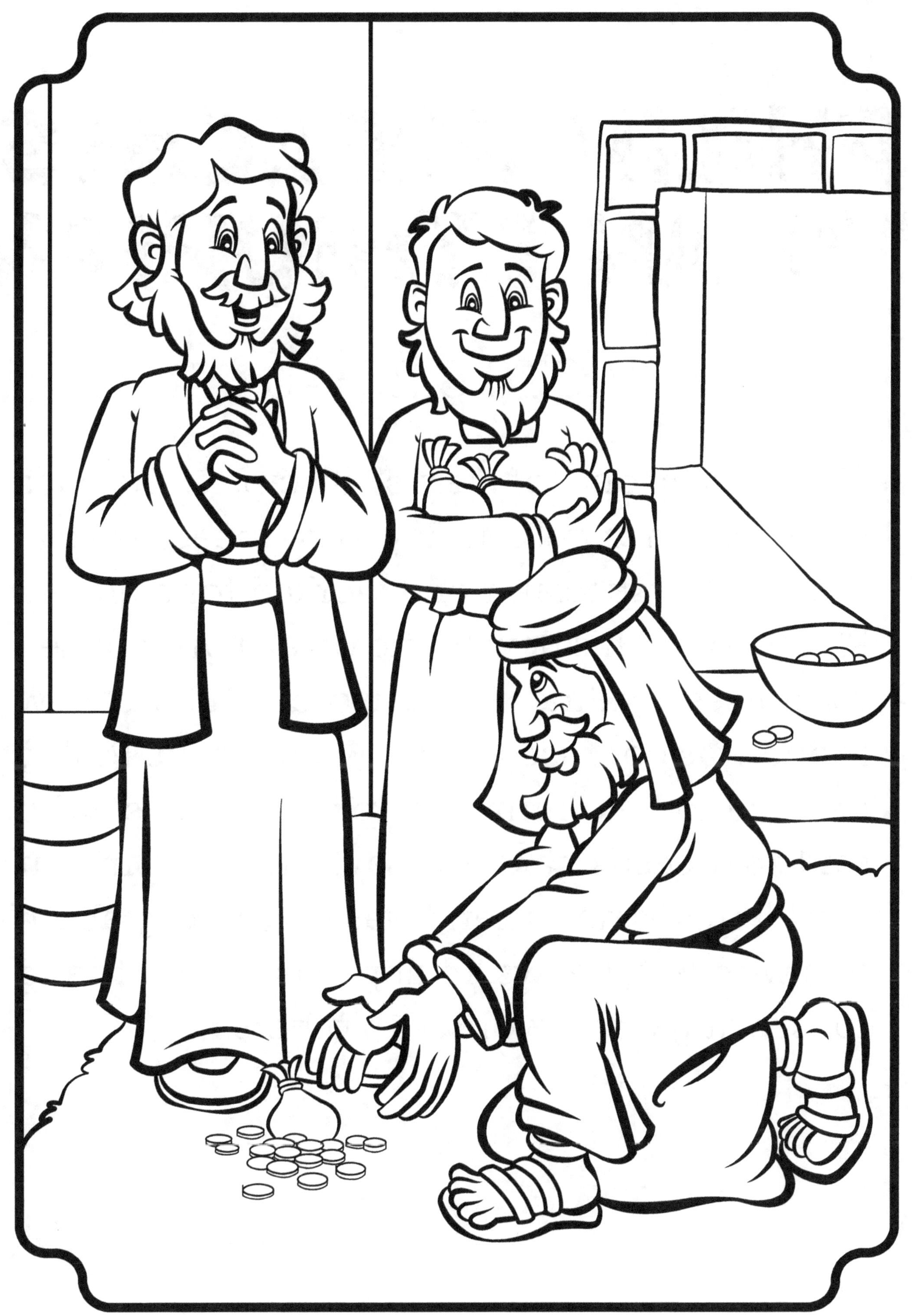

# PHiLiP PREACHES TO AN ETHiOPiAN

## ACTS 8:26-40

Phillip was one of Jesus' disciples. He was visited by an angel one day to go meet a special friend. This special friend worked for a queen! Phillip found his new friend on a chariot pulled by horses reading God's word. Phillip's new friend was confused about what it said. Phillip decided to help him! Phillip said, "God's word said that Jesus came to save us all from our sins!" Phillips new friend was very happy about this wonderful news! Phillip was a good friend for sharing God's word with others.

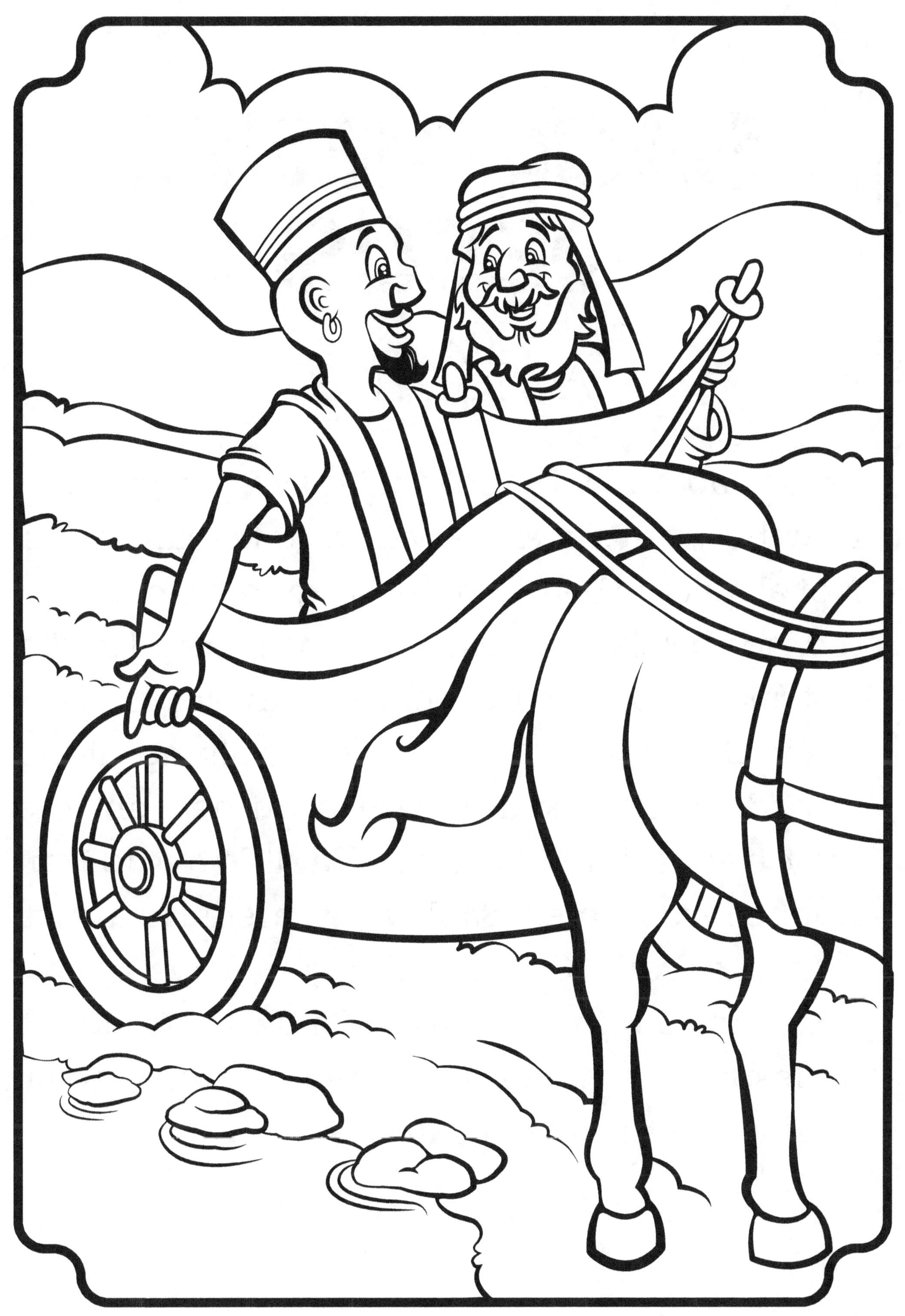

# SAUL MEETS JESUS

## ACTS 9:1-19

Jesus had many friends that loved to talk about how he went up to heaven to take care of us. Not all people believed this! A man named Saul did not believe in Jesus as God's Son! He did not like people who believed in Jesus! This made Jesus sad. As Saul was walking along a road, Jesus talked to him from heaven in a very bright light! He said, "Saul! Why do you not believe in me?" Saul was scared! He asked, "Who are you?" Jesus said, "I am Jesus!" Jesus talked to Saul from heaven! Saul then believed in Jesus and shared the story of Jesus with all he knew! Jesus loved Saul!

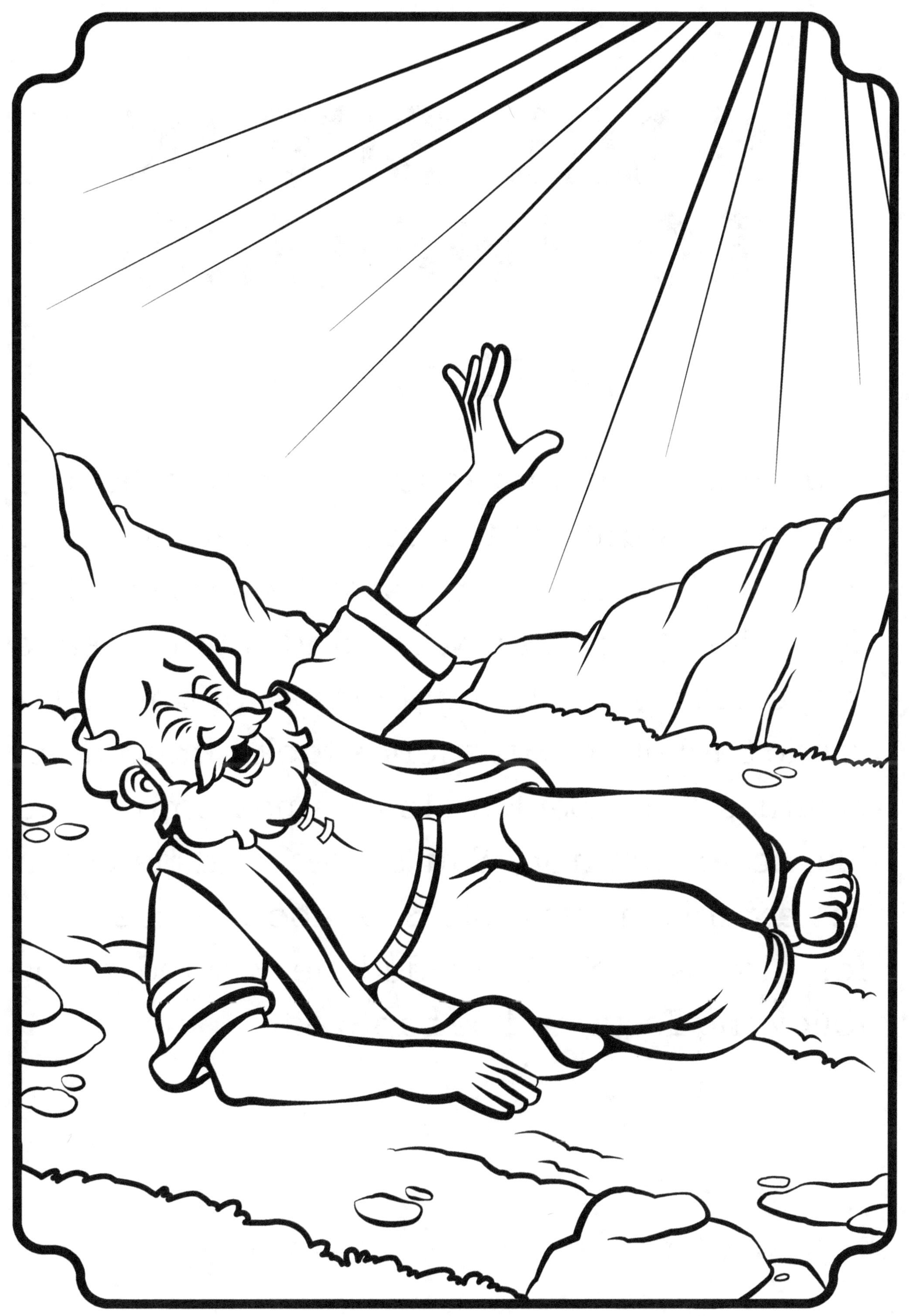

# SAUL SPEAK TO ANANIAS

## ACTS 9:10-19

Saul met Jesus on a road and Jesus talked to him in a bright light. Jesus told Saul to go to town and meet a man named Ananias. After Jesus left, poor Saul was blind! Blind means you cannot see. The light was so bright that it made Saul blind. His friends took him to meet Ananias. Once Saul got to Ananias, something like scales fell from Saul's eyes, and he could see again! Ananias told Saul about Jesus' love for him, and Saul decided he wanted to be following Jesus and be baptized!

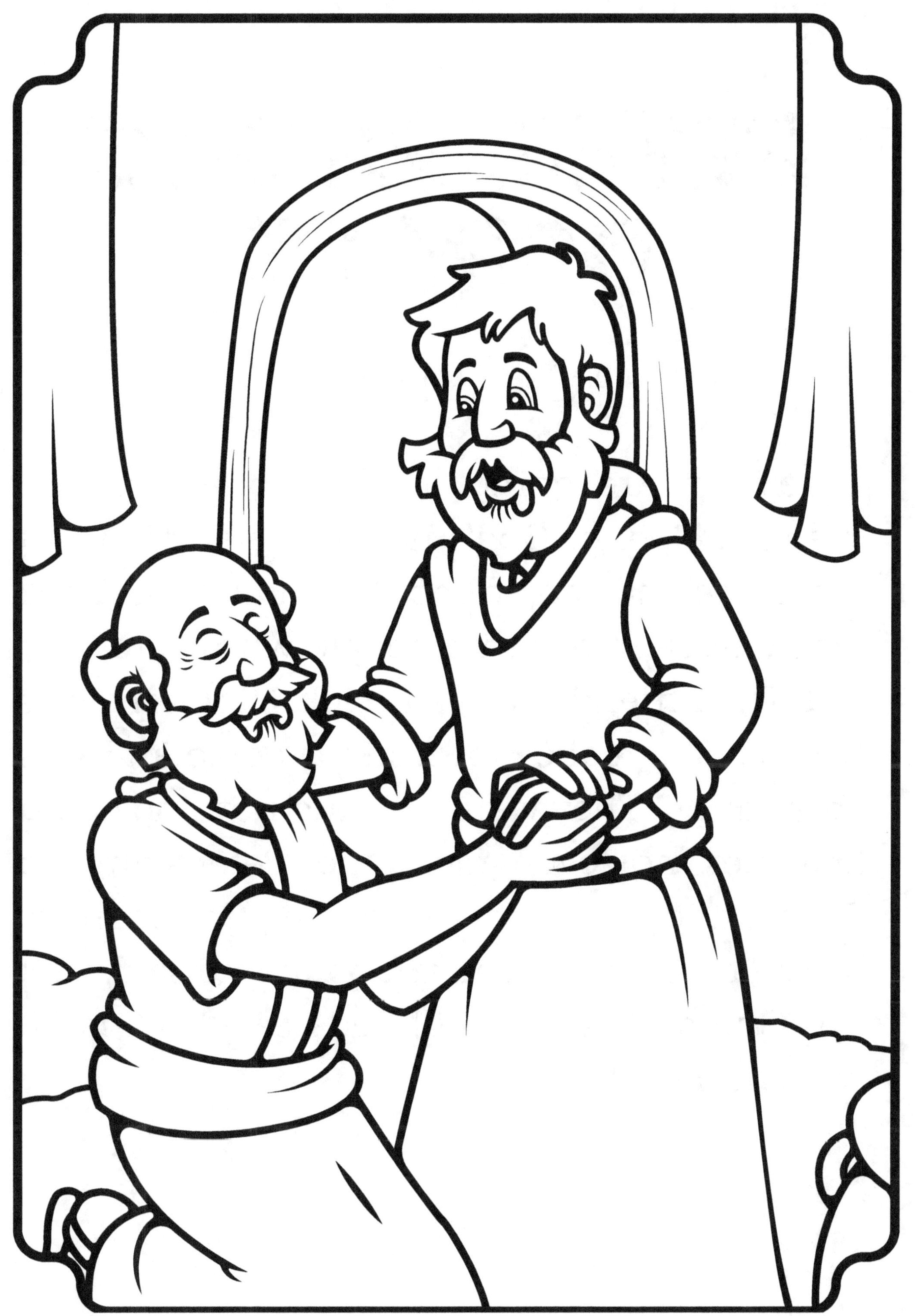

# PETER RAISES DORCAS

## ACTS 9:32-43

Today we are going to talk about another special helper of God's named Peter. He went around telling people about Jesus just like Paul! One day, he met some people who were very sad. Their friend was really sick. Her name was Dorcas. She made clothes for people and was very caring. They were sad, and nothing could help her, not even medicine! Peter came to Dorcas and prayed for her, asking God to make her better. Peter looked at Dorcas and said, "Get up!" Guess what? She did! God healed Dorcas! It was a miracle!

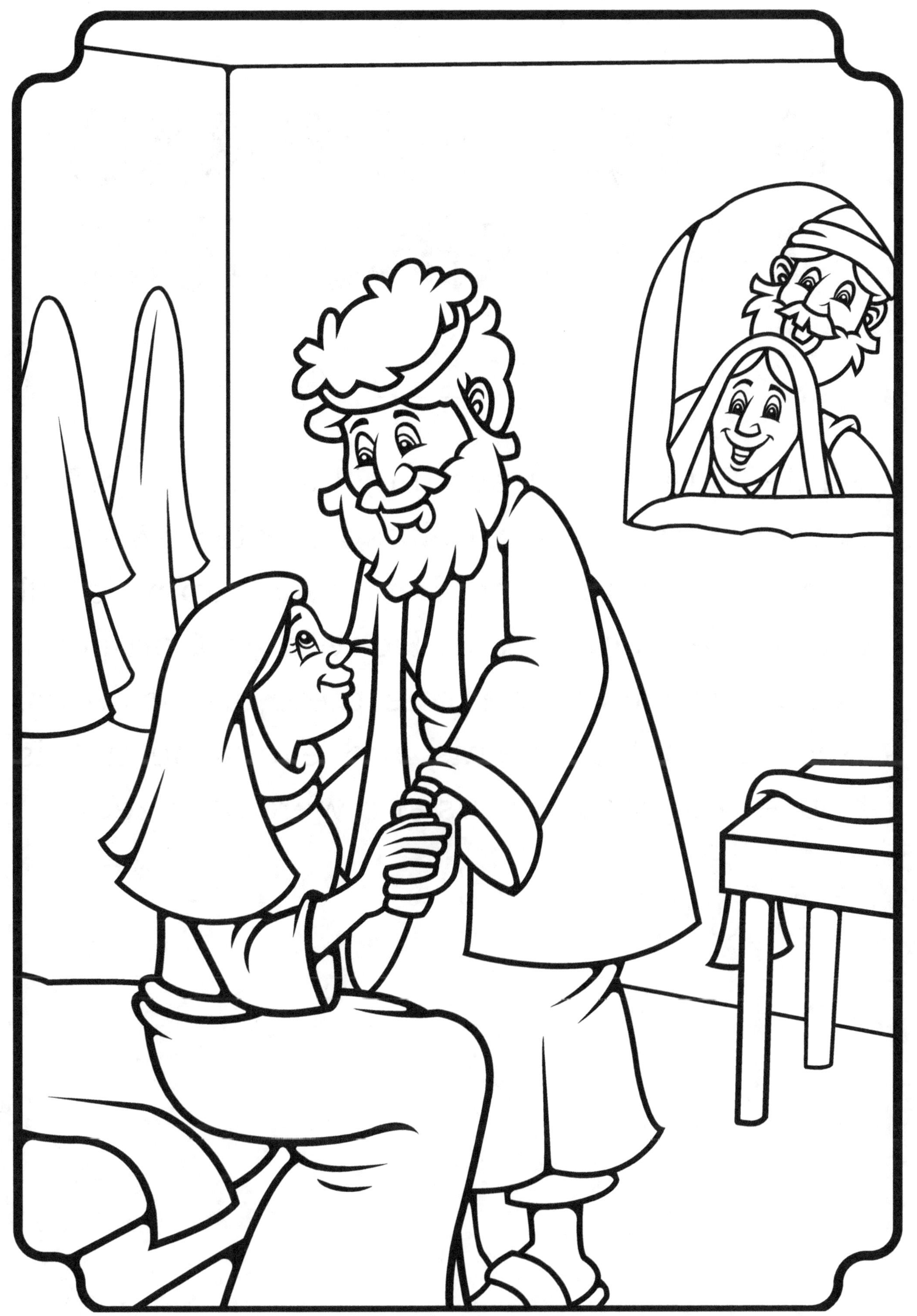

# PETER SPEAKS TO CORNELIUS

## ACTS 10:1-48

While Peter was traveling, he met a soldier named Cornelius. Cornelius did not know about Jesus, the Son of God. Peter was happy to tell the soldier about Jesus. He went to Cornelius' house, and told everyone there about Jesus. Guess what? Cornelius and everyone in his house believed in Jesus and were baptized!

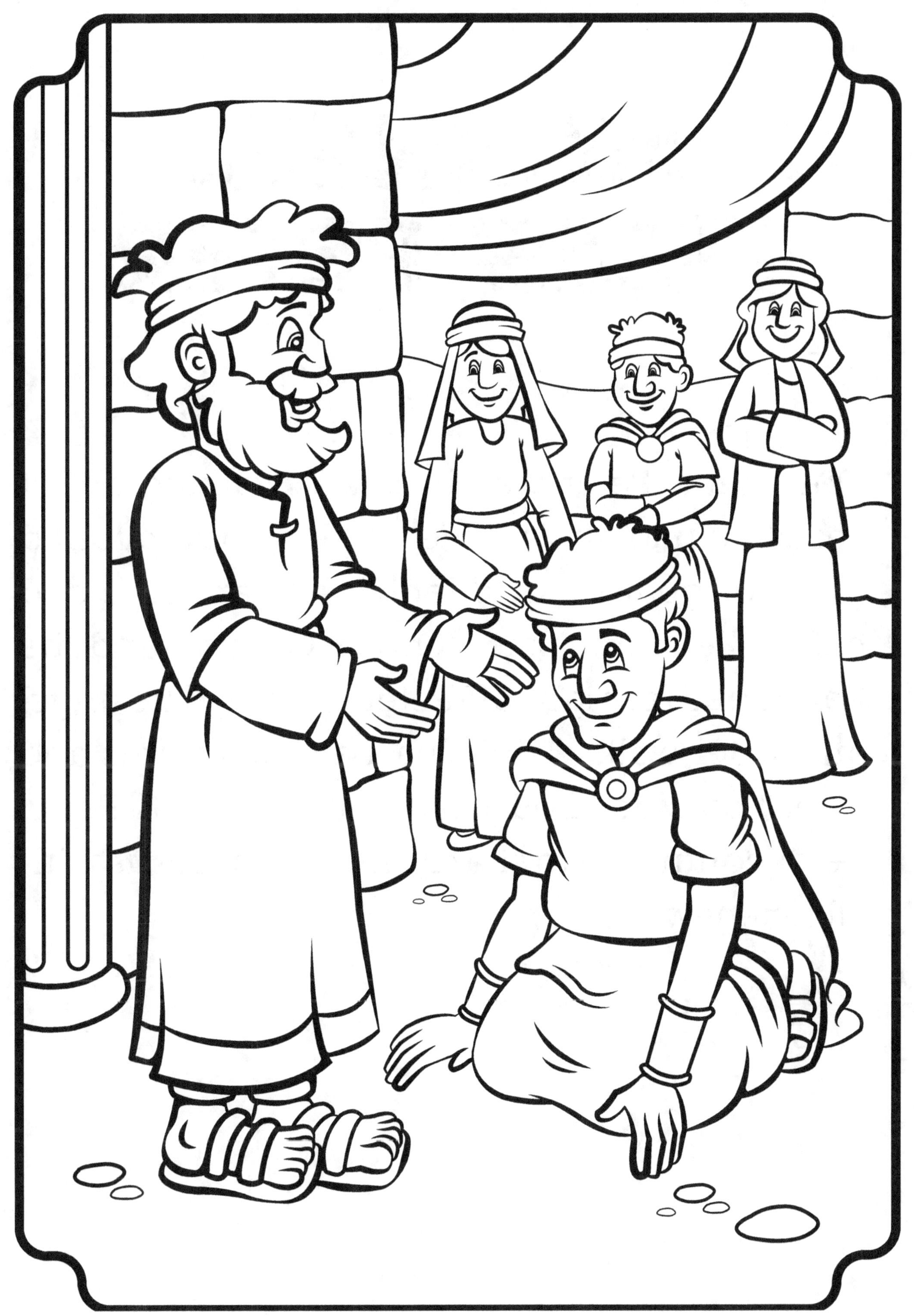

# AN ANGEL FREES PETER

## ACTS 12:1-19

Our friend Peter was in jail for talking about Jesus. While in jail, Peter slept, handcuffed to two guards. Suddenly, an angel stood before Peter and said, "Quick! Get up!" and the handcuffs fell right off Peter's wrists! The angel and Peter walked right past all the guards and safely outside. God was taking care of Peter. Peter continued to share the story of Jesus with all he knew.

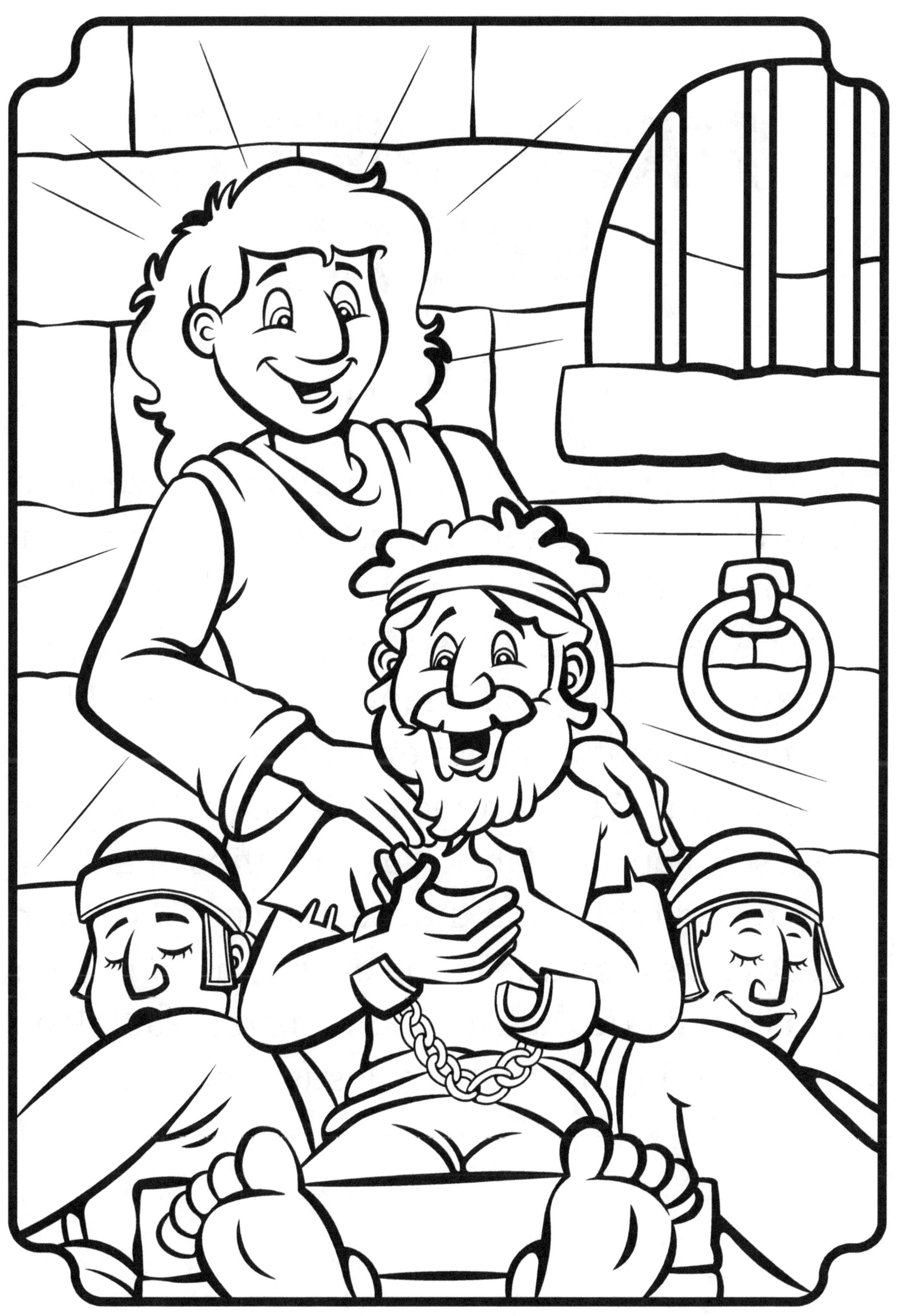

# PAUL MEETS LYDIA

## ACTS 16:11-15

What is the name of the man that we have been talking about? Saul! Guess what? After Saul became a Christian, he changed his name to Paul! After Saul changed his name to Paul, he became a very good friend to Jesus. He liked to speak about Jesus to everyone he met! One day, he met a lady named Lydia down by a river. She sold purple fabric and clothes. Paul sat down and told Lydia that Jesus was God's Son and that he died and came back to life again for us all! Lydia heard this and believed Paul. Paul loved telling others about Jesus, God's son.

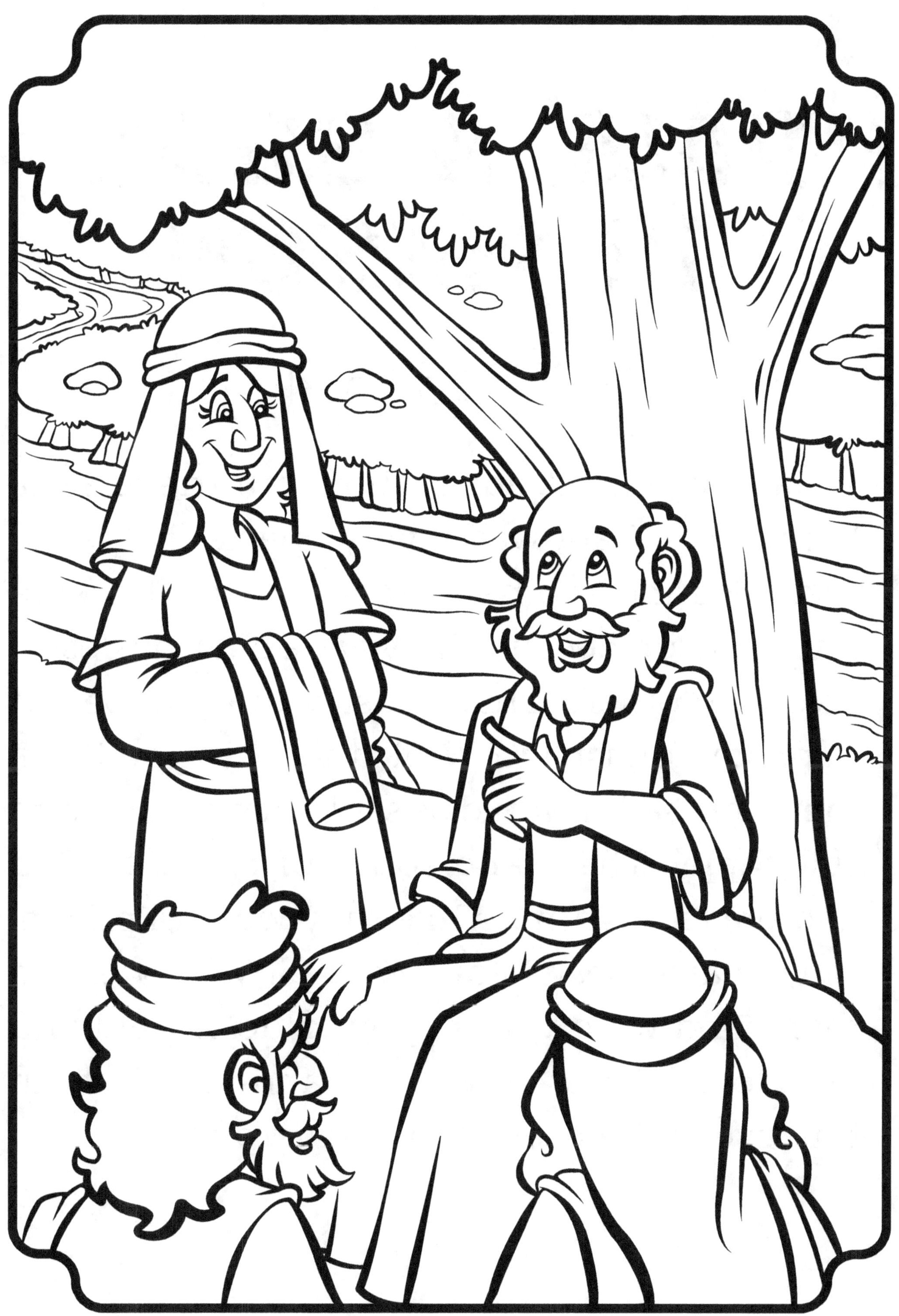

# PAUL & SILAS IN PRISON

## ACTS 16:16-40

Today we will talk again about our friend Paul. Remember, Paul was a very special helper to Jesus. He and another helper named Silas were put in prison because they were sharing Jesus' love with others. That is a silly thing to be put in prison for, isn't it? While there, do you think they were sad? I would be sad! But no, they were still happy! They sang songs of praise to God and prayed to him. While they were in prison, they shared Jesus' love with all who were in there, and were very happy to do it! Paul and Silas loved Jesus very much and talked about him everywhere, even in a scary prison!

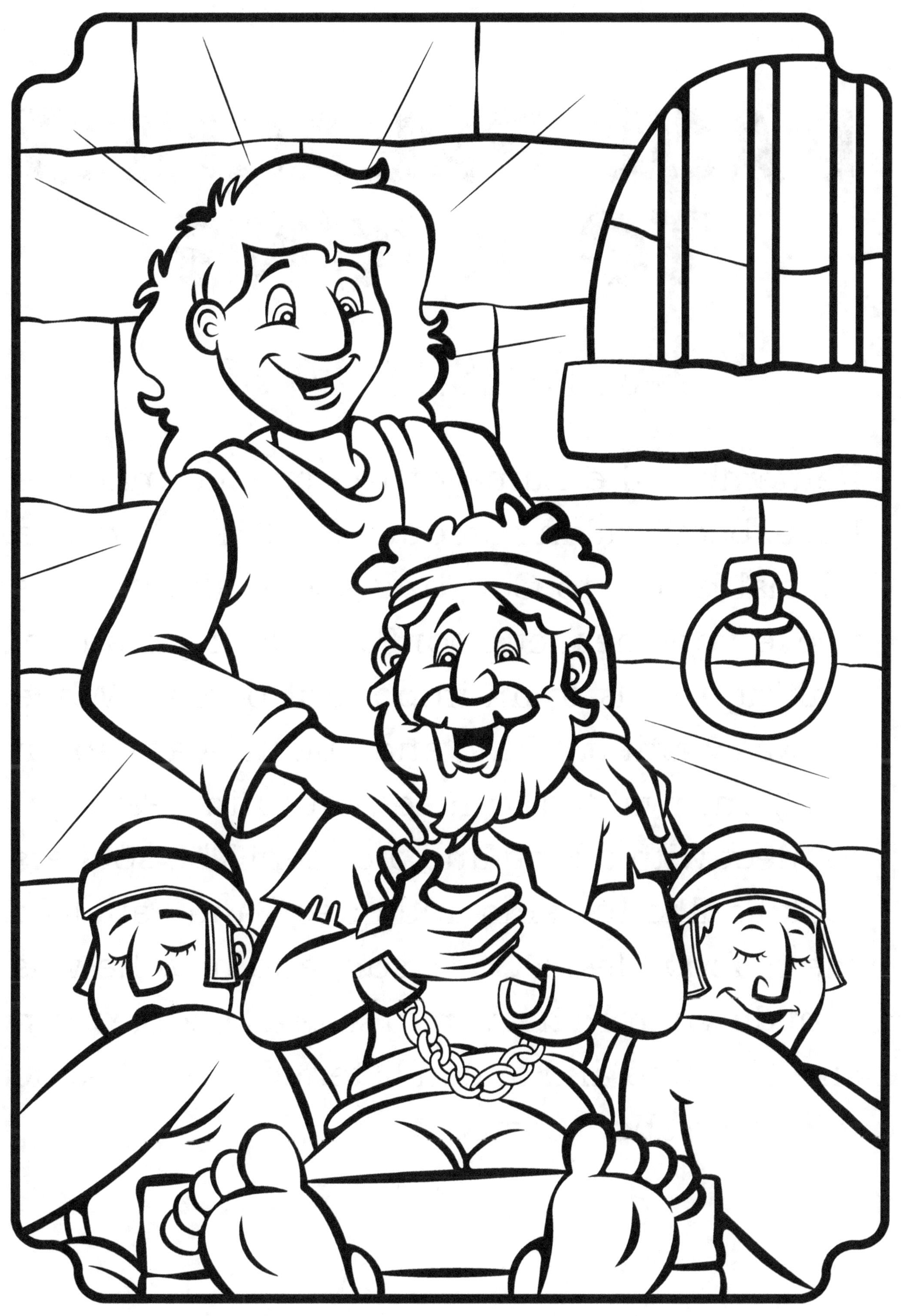

# PAUL PREACHES TO A KING

## ACTS 25:13-26:32

Remember the name of the special man we have been talking about? Paul! Paul was a special helper to God, and spoke about Jesus to everyone he met! Poor Paul was in jail again, waiting to talk to an important person. While he was waiting, a king and queen heard about Paul, and wanted to meet with him! Paul got to meet with a king and a queen! The soldiers took Paul to the king and queen and Paul told them about Jesus God's son, and how he was sent down from heaven to save all people from sin. The king and queen listened to Paul as he told them about Jesus.

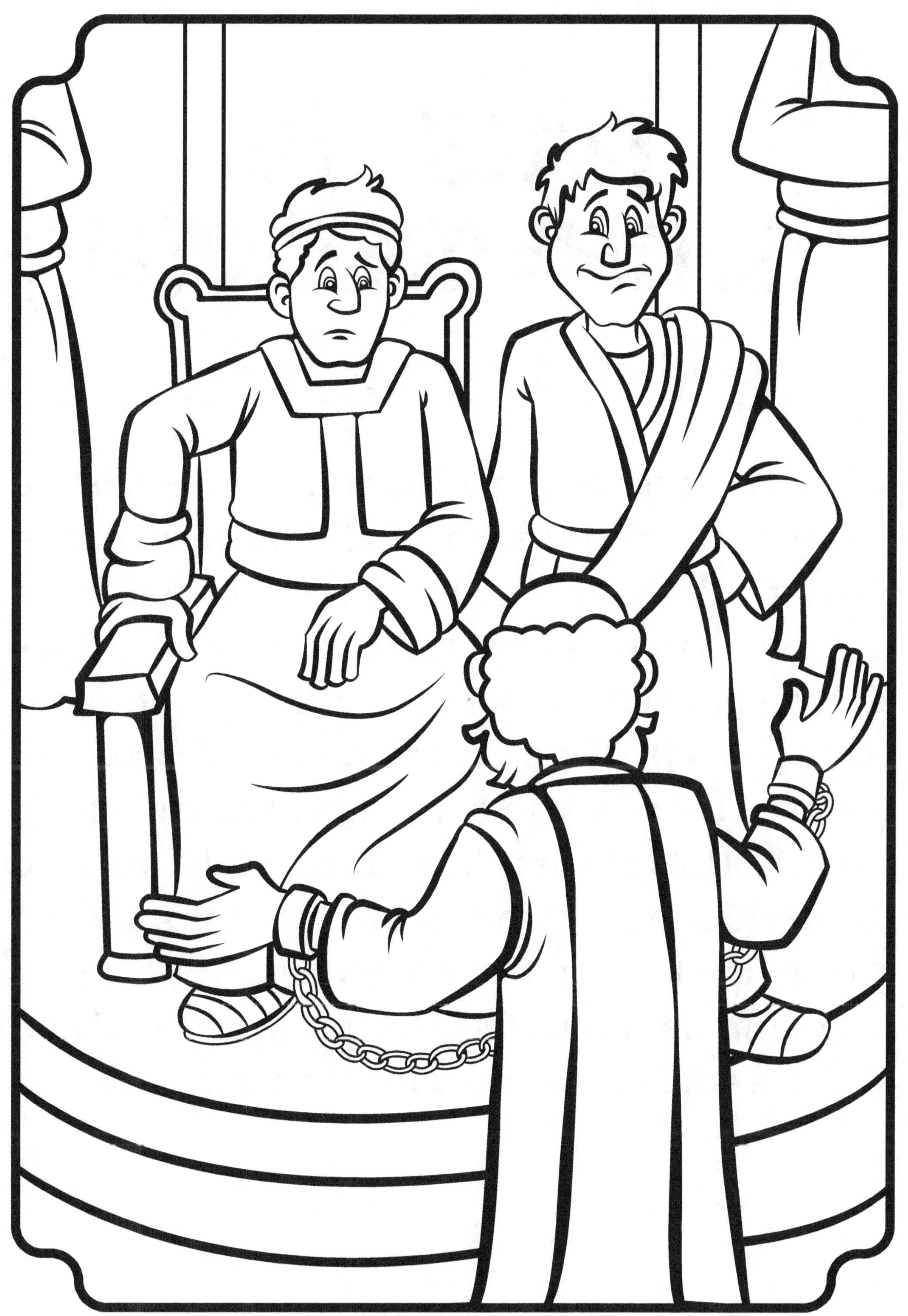

# PAUL iS SHIPWRECKED

## ACTS 27:1-44; 28:1-6

Paul was busy telling all people about Jesus. He got onto a ship to sail to another town where he could talk about Jesus. Paul was worried about sailing in the sea because he knew a storm was coming. Once on board, it started to thunder and get dark. The storm came over the sea and caused big waves to crash against the boat. Oh no! Paul told the people not to be afraid, because God would take care of them. The ship crashed upon the land and broke, but everyone inside the ship was protected. God protected Paul and others when the storm crashed their ship.

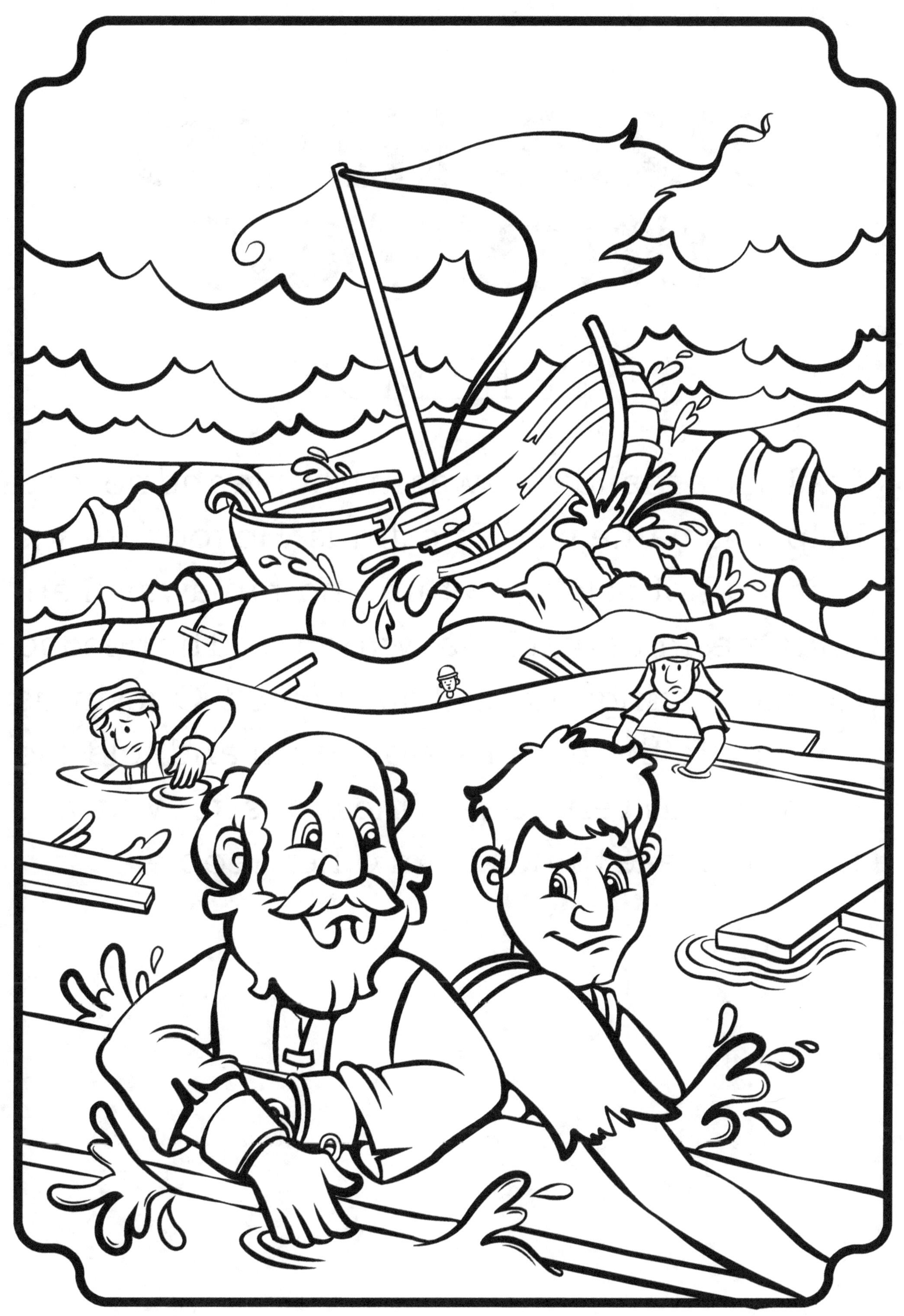

# PAUL HELPS ONESIMUS

## PHILEMON

Paul had a friend who was in trouble and needed help. His name was Onesimus. He took things that did not belong to him and ran away. Paul told Onesimus that it was wrong, and he needed to make things right. Paul helped Onesimus go back to the man he stole from and told the man he was very sorry. Onesimus knew it was wrong to take things from other people.

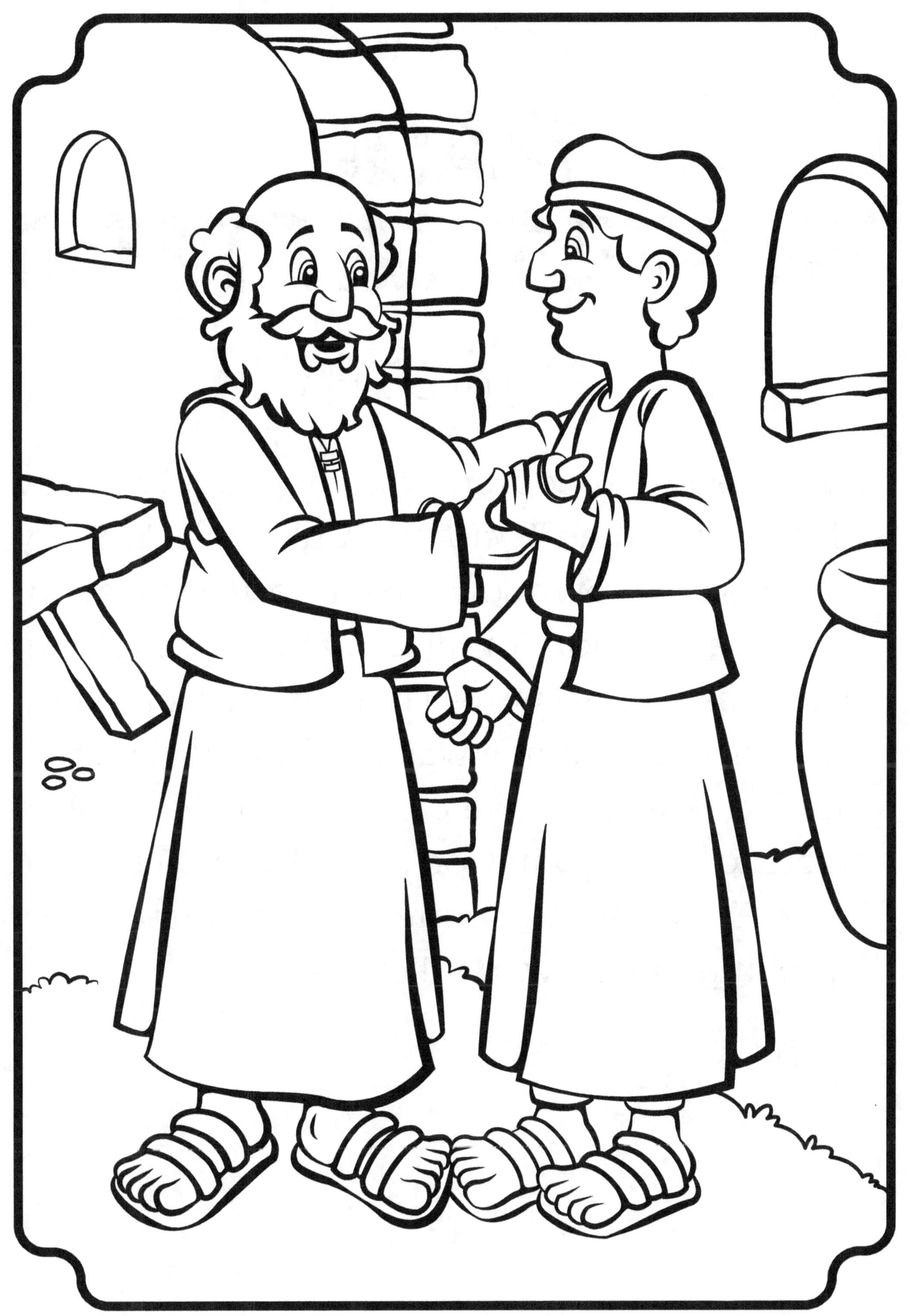

# PAUL WRITES LETTERS

## 2 TIMOTHY

Paul liked to encourage his friends, especially his friend named Timothy. Paul loved Timothy like he was his own son. One time, Paul was sent into a dark prison for talking about Jesus. Paul used this time to write Timothy a letter telling him how important it was to follow Jesus, even when it was hard. We can read the letter Paul wrote to Timothy in God's word, the Bible! Paul loved Timothy, and wanted to encourage him by telling him how to follow Jesus.

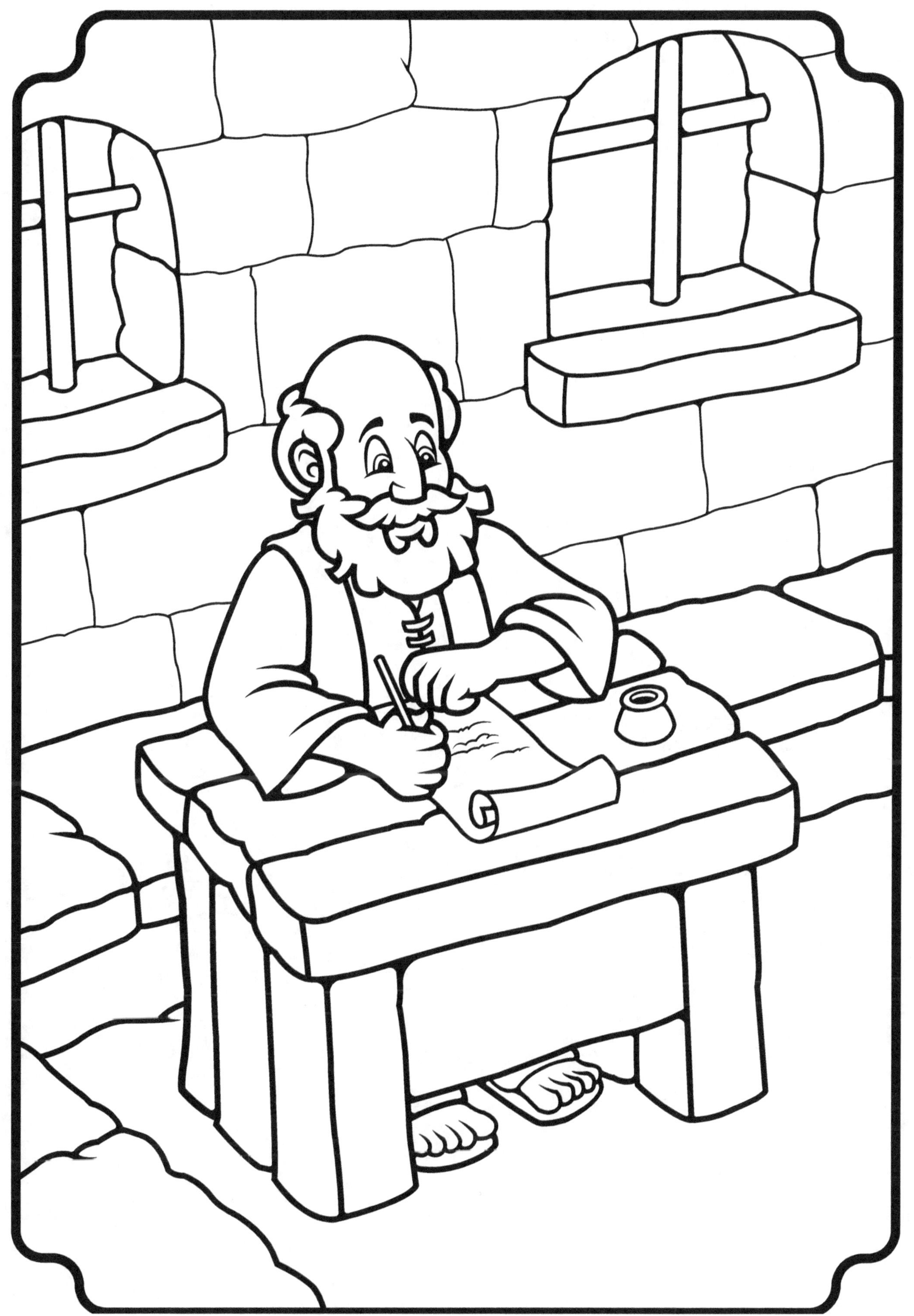